C000273461

DIVINE
INTERVENTION
in days of
DECLENSION

BELFAST, NORTHERN IRELAND
GREENVILLE, SOUTH CAROLINA

DIVINE
INTERVENTION
in days of
DECLENSION

AN EXPOSITION OF THE
BOOK OF JUDGES

by
IAN R K PAISLEY

DIVINE INTERVENTION *in days of* DECLENSION
© Copyright 2002 Ian R K Paisley

All rights reserved

ISBN 1 84030 120 1

Ambassador Publications
a division of
Ambassador Productions Ltd.
Providence House
Ardenlee Street,
Belfast,
BT6 8QJ
Northern Ireland
www.ambassador-productions.com

Emerald House
427 Wade Hampton Blvd.
Greenville
SC 29609, USA
www.emeraldhouse.com

Foreword

Over twenty years ago I preached these messages expounding the Book of Judges.

Recently I got great encouragement and blessing reading this exposition.

The days of the Judges were days of deep and dark declension. How could they be anything else when there was no King and every depraved man did as he pleased in his own wicked eyes?

Those generations paralleled our own generation.

The only hope in this deep and dark human declension is the glorious divine intervention of the Lord Himself.

The Book of Judges is a chronicle of such intervention.

When God moves in, takes up the nobodies, makes them somebodies and turns the tide and brings about glorious deliverances, how wonderful it is!

The God of the Judges is our God. He would stir us up in dedication and prayer to thirst for and expect such divine intervention today.

The days of God's mighty acts are not past. We can expect more and more of them.

Let us heed the good Word of God, and with William Carey, the great missionary pioneer, 'Expect great things *from* God and attempt great things *for* God.'

May the Holy Spirit ignite holy fire in our hearts as we read of God's holy acts of intervention in the past.

May the Covenant God of Israel bless you, dear reader. Yours to serve in the Gospel.

Ian R. K. Paisley
Eph 6: 19+20

IAN R. K. PAISLEY
Eph. 6: 19, 20

Martyrs Memorial Free
Presbyterian Church
356-376 Ravenhill Road,
Belfast, BT6 8GL

21 February, 2002

Contents

Introduction *9*

1. A Bird's-Eye View of the Book *19*
2. The Christophanies of the Book *29*
3. A Consistent Judge, A Resistant Judge, A Persistent Judge *39*
4. Deborah's Song *51*
5. Gideon's Characteristics *69*
6. Faint, Yet Pursuing *79*
7. The Man Who Would Not Go Back On His Word *87*
8. The History, Tragedy and Mystery of Samson *97*
9. The Separation of Samson *105*
10. The Motivation of Samson *113*
11. The Association of Samson *121*
12.. The Confrontation of Samson *129*
13. The Temptation, Degradation and Restoration of Samson *137*
14. Corrupt Morals, Corrupt Religion, Corrupt Priests and Corrupt Faith *147*

Introduction

There are three Books in the Bible which God's people, in this age of declension and apostasy, should study carefully.

The first of these three Books is Judges, which deals with the *character* of apostasy.

The second Book is Nehemiah, which deals with the *confronting* of apostasy, and the third Book is the little Epistle of Jude, which deals with the *curse* of apostasy.

Apostasy and declension are no new things. We can expect them, because the Bible warns and forewarns us about them, and as this age of grace climaxes to its conclusion with the Second Coming of our Lord and Saviour Jesus Christ, declension and apostasy will be manifested in deeper, darker and more diabolical colours.

There is a guiding principle which we should observe - the nearer apostasy comes to judgment, the more unblushing and blaspheming and defying that apostasy and declension will be.

Now, the book of Judges teaches five great lessons, and in this introduction I want to briefly summarise these lessons.

This study is not exhaustive but rather suggestive, and I would suggest various lines of investigation which you can study in your private devotions.

Lesson 1 - The Character of Man

The first lesson is the character of man. Man is seen here in all his debauchery, villainy and depravity.

To listen to some preachers today one would think that when man fell he just broke his little finger, and all he needs is a little hospitalisation. It is not hospitalisation which man requires, it is regeneration. He is totally, absolutely and altogether ruined. Other preachers have the crazy idea that everything about man is depraved as the result of the fall, except his will, and somehow or other the will of man escaped the depravity and corruption of the Fall. What total and utter nonsense! Man is fallen in his heart, fallen in his conscience, fallen in his mind, fallen in his will. He is totally, completely and absolutely fallen. *'The heart is deceitful above all things, and desperately wicked, who can know it?'*

There is no book in the Bible which delineates the character of man - man fallen, man corrupt, man debased, man debauched, man depraved - like the Book of Judges.

When you study the Bible you will find that there are six great apostasies in the Book. Mark them carefully. Six, of course, is the number of man; it is the number of failure; it is the number of depravity.

The Angelic Apostasy

The first apostasy we are told about in the Bible is the angelic apostasy. You will find that in Jude 6, *'And the angels which kept not their first estate, but left their own habitation, He hath reserved in everlasting chains under darkness unto the judgment of the great day.'* Apostasy means 'to depart' - 'to leave your first estate' - 'to deviate from the first foundation' - 'to decline'. The first apostasy in the Bible, the angelic apostasy, the fall of angels, is a most interesting study. Who are the demons on earth today? Are they fallen angels? This is a question worthy of careful consideration in the Word of God.

The Adamic Apostasy

The second apostasy is the Adamic apostasy, the fall of Adam.

The Antediluvian Apostasy

Thirdly, we have the antediluvian apostasy, which took place before the Flood, when the world was filled with violence. *'And as it was in the days of Noe, so shall it be also in the days of the Son of Man.'* (Luke 17:26)

The Sodom Apostasy

The fourth apostasy - Jude 7, is the apostasy of Sodom and Gomorrha.

The Israel Apostasy

The fifth apostasy is Israel. The apostasy of Israel is three-fold -

(i) in the wilderness;

(ii) in the land;

(iii) back in the land. The nation of Israel writes and emblazons across the world 'Apostasy! The apostasy of Israel!

The Church Apostasy

The sixth apostasy is the apostasy of the church, and that is foretold in the New Testament. The final apostasy of the Church is seen in Revelation 17. The great harlot church is not depicted in isolation but in association as *The Mother of harlots and abominations of the earth'*. So we have the character of man taught in this Book in all its loathsome and hateful nature.

Lesson 2: The Compassion of God

The second great thing we have in this Book is the compassion of God. I know no other Book in the Bible which reveals the wonderful mercy, the infinite longsuffering, the tenderness of Divine love, the almightiness of Divine grace, than this Book of Judges. God says in chapter 2:1, *'I will never break my covenant with you.'* God's covenant cannot be broken by man's sin. Salvation cannot be forfeited by man's guilt. When God saves a man, thank God He saves him for ever. There is no breaking of God's everlasting covenant. It is ordered in all things, and sure.

If you want a comment on the compassion of God in the Book, turn to Nehemiah 9, *'Thou art a God ready to pardon.'* In this Book of Judges we have the revelation of a God ready to pardon. How wonderful, amidst the apostasy and declension, the sin and stubbornness and obstinacy of a wicked people, God does not change. Jesus Christ is the same yesterday, today and for ever.

Lesson 3: The Cry of the People of God

Thirdly, this Book teaches the lesson of the cry of the

people of God. Five times in this Book the people cry unto the Lord. Let us glance at them.

(i) Chapter 3:9, *'And when the children of Israel cried unto the Lord.'*

(ii) Chapter 3:15, *'But when the children of Israel cried unto the Lord.'*

(iii) Chapter 4:3, *'And the children of Israel cried unto the Lord.'*

(iv) Chapter 6:7, *'And it came to pass when the children of Israel cried unto the Lord.'*

(v) Chapter 10:10, *'And the children of Israel cried unto the Lord.'*

The Holy Spirit has His numbers right. Five times in the Book we read *'The children of Israel cried unto the Lord.'* Why five times? Because five is the number of grace. *'Let us come boldly unto the throne of grace.'* Hebrews 4:16, It has the significance of grace, If anyone else had been writing this Book they would never have seen to it that there were just five mentions of five great cries unto the Lord, but men did not write this Book! God told its human author what to write. The Bible is always right, and it is always right in its numbers.

One of the great demonstrations of the divine integrity and originality of this Book is its consistent use of numbers. It has a numerical divinity.

Lesson one, the character of man; lesson two, the compassion of God; lesson three, the cry of the people, and before I continue, let it be said that this country will be saved when God's people cry unto the Lord. Marshal the forces of prayer! To your knees, people of God! There never was a day in the history of the people of God when they cried unto God that He did not hear them, and God is the same today. Let us then cry unto the Lord!

Lesson 4: The Choice of the Deliverer

In chapter 2:16-19 we read that God raised up judges. If you have a marginal reference Authorised Version Bible you will find that the word 'judges' is the word 'saviours'. That is what it means. God raised up saviours. These saviours whom He raised up, in the circumstances of their lives, are types of the Lord Jesus. No human person in the Bible is a type of Christ in His character, because man has fallen and sin has polluted him, but many Bible personages are types of Christ in their circumstances.

We could illustrate that briefly in Samson. What did Samson do when his enemies thought they had defeated him? He rose up early and put the pillars and the doorposts and the gates of Gaza upon his shoulders and carried them to the top of the hill.

Jesus Christ burst the gates of the Gaza of Hell, and carried the smashed gates of the enemy's citadel to the top of the Hill Calvary and shouted, 'It is finished!' and the work of Divine redemption was accomplished for evermore.

They are types of Christ only in their circumstances, and you will find there are twelve judges in the Book. Of course, there must be twelve, because twelve in the Bible is the number of government. We have the twelve sons of Israel, making up the twelve tribes of Israel. We have the twelve Apostles of the Lamb. We have the twelve foundations of the City. We have the twelve gates to the City. The Bible is filled with twelves. It is the number of government.

Thirteen in the Bible is the number of apostasy, because it is one more than divine government, and of course it signifies rebellion.

If you count the judges accurately you will find thirteen, but one of them is an apostate judge, as we shall see.

In chapter 3:9-11 we find the first of these judges, Othniel. He is mentioned in three Books of the Bible. Three is the number of completion. Othniel comes from the tribe of Judah. He is mentioned in Joshua, in Judges and in 1st Chronicles.

The second judge, Ehud, is found in chapter 3:12-30.

The third judge, Shamgar, is in chapter 3:31.

The fourth judge, Barak, is in chapters four and five.

The fifth judge, Gideon, you will find in chapters six to nine.

The sixth judge, Tola, is in chapter 10:1,2.

The seventh judge, Jair, is in chapter 10:3-5.

The eighth judge, Jephthah, is in chapters eleven and chapter 12 up to verse 7.

The ninth judge, Ibzan, is in chapter 12:8-10.

The tenth judge, Elon, is in chapter 12:11,12.

The eleventh judge, Abdon, is in chapter 12:13-15.

The twelfth and last judge, Samson, is in chapters thirteen to sixteen.

You ask me 'Who was the apostate judge?' Turn to chapter 8:29, '*And Jerubbaal, (or Gideon) the son of Joash went and dwelt in his own house. And Gideon had threescore and ten sons of his body begotten: for he had many wives. and his concubine that was in Shechem, she also bare him a son, whose name he called Abimelech.*' Abimelech was the apostate. He was the illegitimate. He did not have the proper genealogy. He did not come of the proper line. He was a child of the flesh, and what did he do? Look at chapter 9:5. '*He slew his brethren the sons of Jerubbaal, being threescore and ten persons, upon one stone*' - with one exception, the young boy Jotham. Abimelech was a destroyer of the Royal line. He was an apostate, and as we continue to study this Book we will see his end.

So much for the choice of the Deliverer.

God's man is never elected. God's man is always selected. Do you get it? A leader in the church cannot be elected. Of course, the people of the congregation can elect a minister. If they are guided by the Holy Spirit he should be the man that God has already selected, but many a congregation has elected a minister and he has not been a leader at all, because he wasn't God's man. You can vote for a preacher and a minister, but you cannot vote for a leader. God makes leaders in the church. He takes the weak things, the despised things, the things that are not, to bring to nought the things that are, that no flesh should glory in His presence.

Lesson 5: *The Confounding of the Enemy*

The fifth lesson is the confounding of the enemy. We have the character of man; the compassion of God; the cry of the people; the choice of the deliverer; and finally we have the confounding of the enemy.

I am not talking about the conquering of the enemy, I am talking about the utter confounding of the enemy. Oh, you can conquer and not confound, but confounding comes when the enemy is taken totally and absolutely by surprise, when by some simple thing in the hand of man, God creates a miracle.

We have miracles in this Book - seven of them.

(i) We have the *dagger of Ehud,* the left-handed man, in Judges 3, a most interesting story as we shall see. We ought to study all the left-handed men in the Bible, and ponder why God speaks of His Own left hand. Oh, yes, there is a lot in the Bible about the left hand of God. Find out about His left hand.

(ii)There is the *oxgoad of Shamgar.* Who would have thought that a poor herdsman with an oxgoad could have delivered the whole nation? God takes the weak things, the despised things, the things that are not.

(iii) We have the *nail of Jael,* the woman with the hammer and the nail who brought great deliverance to Israel.

(iv) The *pitchers, torches and trumpets* of the three hundred chosen men of Gideon.

(v) A *piece of a millstone* which a woman threw from the city wall and killed the apostate Abimelech.

(vi) The *mispronunciation of a name* - the name Shibboleth or Sibboleth, which identified the enemies of God.

(vii) Samson's hold on the *jawbone of an ass* and the slaughter of the Philistines.

What does this teach us? That it is *'not by might nor by power, but by My Spirit, saith the Lord.'*

Is it not interesting that the Holy Spirit again has His numbers right? Seven times (the number of perfection) we read about the Spirit of God in this Book. Let me give them to you.

(i) Chapter 3:10, *'The Spirit of the Lord came upon him.'* (Othniel).

(ii) Chapter 6:34, *'But the Spirit of the Lord came upon Gideon.'* If you look in the margin you will find that it is 'clothed Gideon'.

(iii) Chapter 11:29, *'Then the Spirit of the Lord came upon Jephthah.'*

(iv) There are four references to the Spirit of God in the life of Samson.

Chapter 13:25, *'And the Spirit of the Lord began to move him at times in the camp of Dan between Zorah and Eshtaol.'* Note the place carefully, because there is another great historical event which took place in the life of Samson in that very place. The places of Scripture are important.

(v) Chapter 14:6, *'And the Spirit of the Lord came mightily upon him.'*

(vi) Chapter 14:19, *'And the Spirit of the Lord came upon him.'*

(vii) Chapter 15:14, *'And the Spirit of the Lord came mightily upon him.'*

Seven times the Spirit of the Lord comes upon men. *'It is not by might nor by power, but by My Spirit, saith the Lord.'*

Note these lessons. Meditate upon them. Learn their truths, because they are the epitome of the Book and the foundation of the entire Inspired Chronicle of the Judges - the character of man, the compassion of God, the cry of the people, the choice of the deliverer, and the confounding of the enemy.

1

A BIRD'S-EYE VIEW
OF THE BOOK

In the Introduction we saw the five great lessons of the Book. Now we want to take a bird's-eye view of the Book.

The Book of Judges commences with these words, *'Now after the death of Joshua'*, and then it begins to relate certain things which took place before the death of Joshua. There is a parallel between the commencement of Judges and the commencement of the Book of Joshua.

Look with me at Joshua 1:1, *'Now after the death of Moses'*. So the real thrust of Joshua's Book is 'after the death of Moses'. The real thrust of the Book of Judges is 'after the death of Joshua'. Why then does the Holy Spirit tell us about things that happened before Joshua's death, but dates them in this Book as if they happened after he died? The reason is clear: those things that happened before his death laid the foundations for the happenings after his death. With our God there is no past, no present or no future. He is the great I AM. He is not the I WAS; He is not the I WILL BE; He is the I AM, and so this book is written from God's point of view. It is not written from man's point of view.

The Synopsis of the Book

In chapter 2:10 we find the *synopsis of the Book* - *'There arose another generation after them which knew not the Lord, nor yet the works which He had done for Israel.'*

That is the synopsis of the entire Book of Judges - a generation that knew not the Lord, a generation that knew not the wonderful works of the Lord.

The *first section* of the Book is from chapter 1:1 - chapter 2:10.

The *second section* of the Book reveals the *purpose of the Book*. The *purpose* of the Book is seen from verse 11 to verse 23, where you will find how God raised up judges to give deliverance, to smite the enemies of God, to call an apostate nation out of apostasy back to truth and righteousness.

When you come to chapter 3, you will find there the *reason of the Book*. Look at verse 2, *'Only that the generations of the children of Israel might know, to teach them war, at the least such as before knew nothing thereof.'* God used the apostasy of Israel, the backsliding of Israel, the declension of Israel to teach the nation how to fight. You remember David said, *'He has taught my fingers to fight.'* So God must teach His people how to do battle against the enemies of the gospel.

Chapter 3:5 through to chapter 16 is the *main part of the Book*. There we have chronicled the deeds of the twelve judges and the one apostate judge Abimelech - thirteen in all; twelve godly men, God-chosen, God-anointed, God-ordained, and the thirteenth. (The number thirteen in Scripture is the number of apostasy. I suppose that is why it has been looked on as an 'unlucky' number. Things have been twisted by superstition as the years have gone by, but there is a reason for them all). Abimelech the king was an apostate.

The *last chapters of the Book* are very interesting. In chapters 17 and 18, and chapters 19 to 21 we are plunged into the very depths of depravity, debauchery and blasphemy. They are the most hideous chapters in all the Bible. They pull away the covering and we see the corrupted heart of man at its worst. Chapters 17 and 18 deal with *perversion* - perverted light, perverted morals and perverted worship - an exact parallel to our day. This is a day of perverted light. This is a day of perverted morals. This is a day of perverted worship.

Chapters 19 - 21 deal with vileness, vengeance and vindictiveness, and they are hideous in their contents and sad in their reading. This is a bird's-eye view of the Book.

Focus on Two Tribes

There are two tribes which come into focus in the last chapter. In these terrible chapters 17 - 21 there is first of all the tribe of Dan, and then follows the tribe of Benjamin. I want you to think on these two tribes because they play a most important part in this Book. One of the great deliverers - a great judge whose biography is unfolded in this Book, is a man called Ehud. He was of the tribe of Benjamin.

The greatest of all the judges was Samson, and he was of the tribe of Dan. Yet though the tribe of Dan produced a Samson, and though the tribe of Benjamin produced an Ehud, and brought great deliverance and victory to Israel, these two

God-chosen, God-blessed, God-ordained tribes went further into apostasy than any of the other tribes of Israel.

This is a sad picture of our own nation today. There is not a nation in this world which has been more blessed than the British nation; there is not a nation that God has delivered more in battles and wars, in conflicts and confrontations, yet today we see the terrible apostasy of our nation, and in spite of all its deliverances our nation seems determined to go as deep down into depravity as she possibly can. What a commentary is this Book on our own day!

Turn to the commencement of the Book, because the Book in microcosm is found in the first chapter. In this chapter we get two opposite characters, and that common theme is delineated all through the Book - God's people and the Devil's crowd; the apostate and the true apostles of God; the men of darkness and the men of light; the men who follow God and the men who rebel against God.

In the first chapter we are presented with two opposite characters, Adoni-Bezek (verses 5-7) and Achsah (verses 12-15). The name Adoni-bezek means 'lord of justice'. He was not, however, a man of justice. He was an impostor. We have heard cries in our own land today from men of blood and men of violence that they want justice. We know it is not justice which they want, rather it is vengeance and blood-shedding. Adoni-bezek was the same. He called himself the 'lord of justice' but he was a man of blood. He was a monster, a beast; he was devilish and diabolical, and in that first chapter you will find what he did to seventy kings. He cut off their thumbs and their great toes.

When the thumb is removed from the hand, the hand loses its grip. When the great toe is removed from the foot the person's balance is lost and they cannot stand. So Adoni-bezek took away both the grip and the balance of the people, so that they were not able to stand before him. They were not able to grip the sword and fight against his tyranny.

This has always been the strategy of the Antichrist, and Adoni-bezek is one of the many types of Antichrist in the Bible. The strategy of the Antichrist is to take away the power of God's people to resist him by taking away their grip upon the sword of the Spirit, which is the Word of God.

A Lesson To Be Learned

How many churches today have lost their grip on the sword of the Spirit! How many preachers today have lost their grip on the sword of the Spirit! There is no battle in the pulpit. There is no war against the Antichrist. The Antichrist prevails!

Then we have the matter of balance. Once the Devil gets God's people knocked off balance they begin riding theological hobby-horses. Many people today are away out on some theological or doctrinal tangent. The great main road of the gospel and the fight for the faith is forgotten while they spend their time attacking men of God who are seeking to fight to the death the enemies of the gospel. God save us, as a people, from losing our balance and going out on some tangent away from the main course of the gospel. God keep us steady on the King's Highway, walking in the way of truth and righteousness!

Now, what happened to these men? They were under Adoni-bezek's table, gathering meat. There are a lot of preachers today and that is all they are doing - gathering meat, just keeping themselves in a job, just maintaining their own bodily strength. The battle for them is over. They are completely defeated and devastated by the enemy.

In this chapter we have *the law of retribution*. There are two verses in the Bible which lay this law on the line. Ecclesiastes 8:12, *'Though a sinner do evil an hundred times, and his days be prolonged, yet surely I know that it shall be well with them that fear God, which fear before Him: but it shall not be well with the wicked, neither shall he prolong his days, which are as a shadow; because he feareth not before God.'*

Isaiah 3:10,11, *'Say ye to the righteous, that it shall be well with him: for they shall eat the fruit of their doings. Woe unto the wicked! Ii shall be ill with him: for the reward of his hands shall be given him.'* The law of divine retribution! Divine retribution may seem to be lame of foot, but it will in the end overtake the fleetest of foot and bring men to judgment.

The Law of Retribution

In the present tragedy of Ulster have you not often despaired that God has not risen sooner to wrath and judgment? If we have eyes to see and hearts to perceive, can we not see retribution overtaking the enemies of this province? Where are the enemies of this province that were so vocal and strong ten years ago? Their names are forgotten and their voices are no longer heard. Why? Because God has overtaken them with retribution. Do not lose heart, my brother. Do not lose faith, my sister. It shall not be well with the wicked, but it shall be well with the people of God, and they shall eat the fruits of their doing.

Old Adoni-bezek had to confess to retribution when his own thumbs were taken off and his own great toes were severed from his vicious and vile body. *'God has so requited me.'*   You will notice that he did not say 'The Lord'.   If you look at chapter 1:2, *'And the Lord said, Judah shall go up,'* you will notice that LORD is in small capitals.   That is Jehovah in the Hebrew.   Adoni-bezek did not know Jehovah. Jehovah was the covenant God of Israel.   The Jehovah of the Old Testament is the Lord Jesus Christ of the New Testament. Her did not know the Christ, but he knew that God had requited him.   The Holy Spirit is very careful in the language which he uses, for the Holy Spirit is absolutely infallible.

What a tremendous contrast we have between Adoni-bezek and Achsah.   Who was Achsah?   She was the bride of the conqueror.   Who was the conqueror?   Othniel.   Of what tribe did he come?   He came of the tribe of Judah.   In that day He became the lion of Judah's tribe and delivered the people - a perfect type of the Lord Jesus Christ.

Achsah is the bride of the conqueror.   Who is the bride of Christ?   The church!   The name Achsah means 'the conqueror of snakes by charming'.   That is a very interesting suggestion. We do not conquer the Devil by our own strength but thank God we have a power, a secret which conquers the Devil.   It is the Blood of the Lamb.   The church of Jesus Christ overcomes the Devil by the Blood of the Lamb and by the Word of their testimony.

You will notice that this bride received a two-fold blessing - she got the blessing of the upper and the nether springs, two wells of water.   One speaks of the Holy Spirit, for the Bible says *'He shall be in us a well of water, springing up into everlasting life.   This He spake of the Spirit that would be given unto them.'*   What is the other well?   The other well is this Blessed Book - the well of salvation, *'Then shall we draw water out of the wells of salvation.'*   So the Bride had a double blessing. The church has a double blessing, the Holy Spirit and the Blessed Book of God.

The Battle of the Book

I want you to notice *where* the battle raged. It raged around the city of Kirjath-sepher (Joshua 1:11). If you have a marginal Bible you will notice that that name means 'the city of the book.' That is where the war is raging - around this Book. That is where the battle is on today. It is the battle of the Book. The bride was the bride of the conqueror of the Book. The church of Jesus Christ is the bride of the Conqueror of this Book. *'And I saw a seven sealed book, and no man could open it, and I wept much,'* said John, *'and then I was told not to weep, for the Lion of the tribe of Judah hath prevailed to open the Book.'* Christ is the Othniel of the New Testament. He is the One who has conquered the City of the Book.

If we go a little further in our survey we will find that this Book is a Book of solemn warnings from God. You will find three of them in the Book. The first one is at Bochim, chapter 2:1-4. The second one is at the Midianite invasion, chapter 6:7-10, and the last one is at the Philistine and Ammonite invasion, chapter 10:10-14. Three solemn warnings! Three in scripture is the number of completion, so there was a perfect warning given by God. What happened? The nation refused the warning, and as a result of that refusal they became a divided people. If you study the Book you will find it is a Book of divisions. Under Othniel and Ehud all Israel - the whole twelve tribes - stood together to fight the battle. Under Barak four tribes stayed away. Division had come. Reuben, Gilead, Dan and Asher, (chapter 5:15-17), did not respond to the trumpet blow which was sounded to call them to battle.

Under Gideon, Ephraim responded with great difficulty, chapter 8:1-3; then under the usurper Abimelech the decay of the whole nation is displayed in chapter four.

When Jephthah came, Ephraim turned against the man of God and met with a most grievous hurt, chapter 12:1-6.

In the great story of Samson the men of Judah were prepared to turn traitor and surrender God's man, Samson, to the Philistines, chapter 15:9-14.

When the church of Jesus Christ does not heed the warning of God it becomes a divided church. Any church which does not walk by the Word of God will be a divided church. They will not unite in the battle. There will be increasing contention within their own ranks. This is the direct result of disobedience to God's warning.

The Great Periods of Peace

There is something I want you to mark very carefully. Although this Book deals with increasing apostasy, yet it records long periods of peace and victory. So let us not think that although this is an apostate age we are not going to have times of refreshing from the presence of God, and times of victory and times of peace.

Look at the invasions in the Book. Eight years under Chu-shan-rish-a-thaim, the children of Israel suffered, chapter 3:8; eighteen years they suffered under Eglon, chapter 3:14; twenty years they suffered under Jabin, chapter 4:3; seven years they suffered under Midian, chapter 6:1; eighteen years they suffered under Ammon, chapter 10:8; forty years they suffered under the Philistines, chapter 13:1.

If we only look on these years of apostasy and declension we are apt to forget the long peaceful years. The Book covers a period of of four hundred and thirty years. Only one hundred and eleven of these years were under the tyranny of the enemy. For three hundred and nineteen years under the judges there was tranquility and peace. Over and over again we read the words, *'the land had rest.'* Chapter 3:1, forty years; chapter 3:30, eighty years; chapter 5:31, forty years; chapter 8:28, forty years. So do not look only on the dark side, look on the bright side. One hundred and eleven years of anarchy, apostasy, declension and evil, but three hundred and nineteen years of peace, joy and rest.

Those long years were a type of the great millennium which is to come. There is going to be a period in this world's history when for a thousand years the Devil will be tied up. I can never understand those people who tell us the millennium is now, for the Devil is certainly not tied up today. He is running around, very busy, but one day he will be tied up in the bottomless pit, and there is going to be a period of rest. In Isaiah 1:26 God says, *'I will restore thy judges as at the first.'* So these periods of rest in Judges are a type of the glorious millennium when the Lord shall reign in righteousness.

We are not children of defeat, we are children of victory. Christ is upon the Throne. The Lion of Judah's tribe, the mighty Othniel, shall win the day. We shall enjoy all the blessings of the upper and nether springs. We shall indeed occupy the City of the Book.

2

THE CHRISTOPHANIES
OF THE BOOK

During these Lord's Day mornings we have been opening up this great Book of Judges. We have looked at it and discovered it is a Book of declension and deliverances. Last Lord's Day we took a bird's-eye view of the Book and made a summary of its contents.

This morning I want to look at a very intriguing subject, the Christophanies, or the pre-incarnation appearances of the Lord Jesus Christ in the Book.

In any study of the Old Testament you will discover that from time to time the Lord appeared unto His people. These appearances have been called theophanies, or appearances, of God, but they are more correctly called Christophanies, because they are really the appearances of the Second Person of the Trinity, because in the wisdom of God from all eternity God ordained that His Son, and His Son alone, should take human form, identify Himself with men and become the only Mediator between God and man, and hence the Saviour of the world. So the pre-incarnation appearances in the Old Testament are appearances of Christ.

There are some things about these appearances which need to be carefully noted.

(i) They were actual appearances. The people did not imagine them; they were not visions or dreams; they were actual appearances of the Lord Jesus Christ.

(ii) They were initiated by God alone. In His sovereignty He chose certain times to visit this earth and reveal Himself miraculously, but actually, to chosen people.

(iii) They all had a special revelation significance. Every time Christ appeared in the Old Testament He wanted to teach a special lesson or to intimate a special event.

(iv) They were largely given to individuals rather than to a great mass of people, although at times Christophanies occurred to the entire nation when gathered together for sacrifice or convocation.

(v) They were intermittent; they did not occur at set times, but they occurred at peculiar and special times.

(vi) They were fleeting, lasting sometimes for minutes, sometimes for a few hours, but never longer.

(vii) They were audible and visible. The voice was heard; the Personage of the Son of God was looked upon. Those who saw, actually saw the Christ. There is no contradiction in that great text, *'No man hath seen God at any time, but the only begotten which is in the bosom of the Father, He hath declared Him,'* because it was Christ (who of course is God) who was seen, but He was always seen in His mediatorial capacity.

(viii) These Christophanies varied in form. There was the form in the burning bush when God spoke to Moses out of the bush. There was the man of God in Judges chapter thirteen, when He said His name was 'Secret'. If you look in the margin of your AV Bible you will see His name was 'Wonderful'. Who is wonderful? The Lord Jesus, *'His name shall be called Wonderful, Counsellor, the Mighty God, the Everlasting Father, the Prince of Peace.'*

(ix) These Christophanies are only linked to the pre-incarnation appearances. No Christophany occurred after the Lord's resurrection, because when He appeared after the resurrection He appeared in the actual body in which He lived upon this earth. We believe in the bodily resurrection of the Lord Jesus Christ, and the same body that was offered on the Cross actually rose from the dead, and in that body He sits at God's right hand.

Now, having laid that foundation, let us turn to this interesting Book of Judges and you will find four Christophanies in its pages.

The first one is in chapter two, *'And an angel of the Lord came from Gilgal to Bochim.'* (v.1) and *'...when the angel of the Lord spake these words unto all the children of Israel'*, (v.4). The terms 'an angel' and 'the angel of the Lord' should be carefully noted. The word 'angel' in the Scripture does not always refer to a celestial being, because the word in the Hebrew and the word in the Greek means 'messenger'. You could read it, *'a messenger of the Lord'* (v.1) or *'the messenger of the Lord'*, (v.4)

'The angel of the Lord encampeth round about them that fear Him....' Ps.34:7. Now our holy fear is not given to angels, our holy fear is given to God alone, but the angel of the Lord is the Lord Himself, and that is why the angel of the Lord and the Lord Himself are used interchangeably in the Old Testament Scriptures.

Let me illustrate it. Turn to Exodus 3:2, - and there you will find the Christophany at the bush - '*And the angel of the Lord appeared unto him in a flame of fire out of the midst of a bush*'; then come to verse 4, '*And when the Lord saw that he turned aside to see, God called unto him out of the midst of the bush.*' So 'the Lord' and 'the angel of the Lord' and 'God' are interchangeable terms, because 'the angel of the Lord' in the Old Testament is the Christ, so when the angel of the Lord appeared it was the Christ, the Messenger of the Covenant, the Minister of the Lord, the One who was appointed Mediator of His people.

Now come to Exodus 32, and you will discover that God said '*Behold mine Angel shall go before thee.*' In the AV, angel is spelt with a capital A, and rightly so, as it refers to Christ Himself. '*Mine Angel shall go before thee: nevertheless in the day when I visit I will visit their sin upon them.*' (v.34). In chapter 33:1 we read, '*And the Lord said unto Moses, Depart, and go up hence, thou and the people which thou hast brought up out of the land of Egypt, unto the land which I sware unto Abraham, to Isaac, and to Jacob, saying, Unto thy seed will I give it: And I will send an angel before thee.*' Not 'an angel' or 'an angel of the Lord' or 'the angel of the Lord' , but just 'an angel'. What happened? In verse 4 we read: '*And when the people heard these evil tidings, they mourned.*' Was not God sending an angel among them? Yes, but He had withdrawn Himself. His own angel, 'the angel of the Lord', had withdrawn, and so it was evil tidings. They were only going to have a celestial being to lead them, and not the Son of God Himself. So it is quite clear that the 'Angel of the Lord' referred to God Himself, the Second Person of the Adorable Trinity, our Lord Jesus Christ.

Turn now to Judges chapter 2: '*And ye shall make no league with the inhabitants of this land; ye shall throw down their altars:*

but ye have not obeyed my voice: why have ye done this? Wherefore I also said, I will not drive them out from before you; but they shall be as thorns in your sides, and their gods shall be a snare unto you. And the people lifted up their voice, and wept.........And they sacrificed unto the Lord.' The interesting thing is this, that the appearances of Christ are always linked to the Cross of Christ. In this first appearance we find that they wept and prayed and sacrificed, for when the Son of God reveals Himself to men He always leads them to the Cross, because the Cross is the climax of Divine revelation, the great 'go' of the gospel, and the apex of the covenant of saving, sovereign and supernatural grace.

There is something else we ought to note, that in all the Christophanies in the Book of Judges there is always the coming afterwards of the Spirit of God. Look at chapter 3:10, after the Christophany of chapter 2, *'The Spirit of the Lord came upon Othniel,.* because the coming of the Spirit of God is linked with the coming of the Son of God. Christ came first, then came the Cross, and then came Pentecost. There is no way to Pentecost in one's life but by knowing Christ, and then by knowing Christ we are led to the Cross, and then from the Cross to the Upper Room for empowerment for service.

The second Christophany is found in chapter 6:11, *'And there came an angel of the Lord, and sat under an oak which was at Ophrah, that pertained unto Joash the Abie-ezrite; and his son Gideon threshed wheat by the winepress, to hide it from the Midianites.'* The oak trees in Scripture are worthy of study, because they represent the Cross of the Lord Jesus Christ. Here we find the Christophany at the oak tree in Ophrah. In verse 12 we read, *'And the angel of the Lord appeared unto him'*, and then there was an offering. *'And Gideon went in, and made ready a kid, and unleavened cakes of an ephah of flour: the flesh he put in a basket, and he put the broth in a pot, and brought it out unto him under the oak tree, and presented it. And the angel of God said unto him, Take the flesh, and the unleavened cakes, and lay them upon this rock, and pour out the broth. And he did so. Then the angel of the Lord put forth the end of the staff that was in his hand, and touched the flesh and the unleavened cakes; and there rose up fire out of the rock, and consumed the flesh and the unleavened cakes. Then the angel of the Lord departed out of his sight. And when Gideon perceived that he was an angel of the Lord, Gideon said, Alas, O Lord God! for because I have seen an angel of the Lord face to face. And the Lord said unto him, Peace be unto thee; fear not: thou shalt not die. Then Gideon built an altar there unto the Lord, and called it Jehovah-shalom; unto this day it is yet in Ophrah of the Abiezrites.'* Notice all the things in relation to the Cross - the oak tree, the rock, the staff. Immediately after this revelation of Christ to Gideon, we read in verse 34, *'The Spirit of the Lord came upon Gideon.'* So the coming of Christ is related to the Cross, and the Cross of Christ is related to the coming of the Holy Spirit. This is exactly what these Christophanies are teaching us There is no way to God but through Christ. There is no way to God but through a crucified Christ. *'We preach Christ crucified.'* But in that Cross and finished work and glorious resurrection we are brought to an Upper Room where the Holy Spirit of God comes down upon His people, enduing them and empowering them to do the work of God and thwart the enemies of the Gospel with the sword of the Lord and of Gideon.

Turn to chapter 10:10, and you will find that the Lord appeared and spoke to them. *'And the children of Israel cried unto the Lord, saying, We have sinned against Thee, both because we have forsaken our God, and also served Baalim. And the Lord said unto the children of Israel, Did not I deliver you from the Egyptians, and from the Amorites, from the children of Ammon, and from the Philistines? The Zidonians also, and the Amalekites, and the Maonites, did oppress you; and ye cried to me, and I delivered you out of their hand. Yet ye have forsaken me, and served other gods: wherefore I will deliver you no more. Go and cry unto the gods which ye have chosen; let them deliver you in the time of your tribulation. And the children of Israel said unto the Lord, We have sinned: do thou unto us whatsoever seemeth good unto thee; deliver us only, we pray thee, this day. And they put away the strange gods from among them, and served the Lord: and his soul was grieved for the misery of Israel.'*

Here we have the appearance of the Lord Himself, when He spoke audibly to them. Immediately after that appearance, we read in verse 29, *'Then the Spirit of the Lord came upon Jephthah.'* Please notice that preceding the Spirit's coming is the Son's coming. The Son said, *'It is needful for me to go away, for if I go not away the Spirit of God will not come,'* In these passages we have the Divine order clearly set forth.

The last great Christophany of the Book is in chapter 13:3, *'And the angel of the Lord appeared unto the woman.'* The message was for separation, for holiness of life, for a repudiation of the world because a Deliverer was to be born. The angel came the second time. *'God speaketh once, yea, twice, but man perceiveth it not.'* The second time the angel of the Lord came and a burnt offering was made to the angel of the Lord. The angel said, *'You will offer it to the Lord',* because He was the Lord Himself. Then they asked His name, *'And Manoah said unto the angel of the Lord, What is Thy name, that when Thy sayings come to pass we may do Thee honour?'* If this had been just an angel, the angel would have said, 'You will not do me honour. There is only one Person that you will honour, and that is God Himself.' But the angel of the Lord did not say that. He just said, *'Why askest thou thus after My name, seeing it is secret?'* (In the margin, as I have already mentioned, it is 'Wonderful'). What happened? Similar to Gideon, they took a kid, a meat offering, and offered it upon a rock unto the Lord, and the angel of the Lord whose name was Wonderful, did wondrous things, verse 19. Is not that lovely? The wonderful Christ does wonderful things. Those of us who are redeemed can say 'He has done wondrously.' In Matthew we read of the 'wonderful things that He did'. Where the Lord is there are wonderful things.

In chapter 13:20, there is an addition to the appearance of Christ. *'When the flame went up toward heaven from off the altar, the angel of the Lord ascended in the flame of the altar.'* Here we have something more, an addition to the appearance of Christ. The first time we have a blessed truth; the second time we have a little more; the third time we have a little more and the fourth time we have more again. That is the way God teaches in His Book, 'Line upon line, precept upon precept, here a little and there a little.' In this last one you will notice that the angel of the Lord ascended to heaven upon the flame, so we not only have the appearance of Christ and the Cross of Christ, but now we have the ascension of Christ.

Let me show you the coming of the Spirit of God. Verse 25, *'And the Spirit of the Lord began to move him* (that is, the child that was born) *at times in the camp of Dan between Zorah and Eshtaol.'* This is very interesting, because the place where the Spirit of God moved Samson at the first, was the place that they buried him. Turn to chapter 16:31, *'Then his brethren and all the house of his father came down and took him, and brought him up, and buried him between Zorah and Eshtaol.'* So in the place where the Spirit of God came upon him, is where they buried him. Buried in faith!

Thank God, every believer who dies is buried in the faith of his glorious birthday. It may be his burial day, but he is buried in the faith of his birthday, which assures a resurrection from the dead. If you study all the appearances of the Lord Jesus Christ in the Old Testament you will find that there is some new truth revealed in each one.

What a wonderful Saviour is Jesus my Lord! May we get to know Him more and more through the study of His Word.

Perhaps you have never set your eyes by faith upon God's well-beloved Son; you are a stranger to His grace, a sojourner in the city of destruction, walking the path of perdition, without God, without Christ and without hope. Let me tell you that you can be saved to-day through faith alone in the Saviour. *'Believe on the Lord Jesus Christ, and thou shalt be saved, and thy house.'* Whosoever comes to Christ He will never cast out. Look, look, look and live for evermore! I trust that both saint and sinner will look to this blessed Christ, the sinner to be saved, the saint to be sanctified, and that as we read the Volume we will look in its Books, because the Saviour said, *'In the volume of the Book it is written of me.'*

3

A CONSISTENT JUDGE,
A RESISTANT JUDGE,
A PERSISTENT JUDGE

We will now look at the first three judges.

The *first one* appears in chapter 3:8, when Chu-shan-rish-a-tha-im king of Mesopotamia overthrew and conquered the children of Israel. Then God raised up Othniel the younger brother of Caleb, to be the first judge to deliver Israel.

The *second one* you will find in the same third chapter, in verse 15, *'Ehud the son of Gera, a Benjamite, a man left-handed.'*

The *third one* is found in the last verse of the third chapter, *'Shamgar the son of Anath.'*

Now these three men are characterised by special attributes. Othniel is characterised by consistency; Ehud is characterised by *resistancy*, and Shamgar is characterised by *persistency*. So we could call Othniel the consistent judge; Ehud the resistant judge, and Shamgar the persistent judge.

The consistent Judge

Let us first of all examine the consistency of Othniel. Turn to chapter 3:2 and if you follow carefully you will find that the purpose of God in allowing the people of God to be overthrown time and time again and then to raise up deliverers and deliverances for them, is recorded in verse 2. *'Only that the generations of the children of Israel might know, to teach them war, at the least such as before knew nothing thereof.'* So the Divine purpose, the Divine objective, the Divine goal of permitting the overthrow of the children of Israel and the raising up of deliverers for them was that they might be taught how to battle, fight, struggle, confront and conquer their enemies.

Reading the history of the Christian Church we are apt to wonder why God allowed the floods of heresy and apostasy to inflict the Church, the Israel of God. We have only to look at the end of the apostolic era and to see how the Church rapidly deteriorated by the introduction of ritual and ceremony, leading to the evolution of what is known in history as Latin Christianity or Vaticanism or Romanism. How the simplicity of the ordinances, the simplicity of the gospel and the fundamental doctrines of revealed Christianity were attacked. After the death of the Apostles it was not long until the entire Christian Church was in the throes of controversy and conflict. Why did the Lord permit it? He permitted it so that the children of God might learn how to use the weapon, the sword of the Spirit, which is the Word of God, and how to come to a clear understanding and to a definitive position on the doctrines of the Bible, the Trinity, the Deity of Christ, the Humanity of Christ and the great doctrines of eschatology, on Romanism, Heaven and Hell, and the Second

Glorious Coming of our great Lord and Saviour, Jesus Christ.

We are apt to ask today, Why is it in this century that God has allowed all Christendom to become apostate, and the pulpits of the majority of Protestant Churches, so-called, to no longer sound forth the old-time religion and the old-time gospel? Why has God permitted it? He has permitted it so that the true people of God, the elect of God, might know how to use the Sword, that they might be militant, strong, fervent, filled with confidence, that they might have a 'thus saith the Lord' upon their lips, and that they might know how to define and defend the great principles of the Gospel. That is the reason revealed in the Book of Judges.

Look at chapter 3:8 - *'The anger of the Lord was kindled.'* It is a sad thing when God kindles His anger against His people. God does kindle His anger against His people. The people of God are not immune from the anger of God. *'Whom the Lord loveth He chasteneth, and scourgeth every son whom He receiveth'.* The Church of Jesus Christ has to come under the lash because of its sin. If ever there was a day when God is angry with His people, surely it is today. That is why there is dearth, darkness and depression. That is why the enemy has come in like a flood. That is why the Church has lost its spiritual effectiveness, its cutting edge for God, because of unjudged sin and compromise, and as a result the enemy has come in and taken over.

For eight years the people of God served the King of Mesopotamia; for eight years they were under the hand of this King, and then God did something. Deliverance at any time is the act of a sovereign God. God must do it.

First comes judgment

Look at verse 10 and you will find how the Lord did it.

This is a very important verse, because it shows the consistency of Othniel. *'The Spirit of the Lord came upon him, and he went out to war.'* You read nothing of the kind! There is something between the coming of the Spirit of God and the battle in which Othniel engaged. What is it? He judged Israel. Before the people of God are fit for the conflict, before they can really battle for the Lord, before they can successfully resist the enemy, judgment must fall upon them. The thing which kindled the anger of God must be put away. What does Peter say? *'Judgment must begin at the house of God, and if it first begin at us.........where shall the ungodly and the sinner appear.'* Until God's Church in this day is prepared to be judged by that very Word of God which in turn will be its own effective weapon in the conflict, it cannot be effectual in the heart of others. There must be judgment.

Would to God the people of God would awaken to judgment and have done with worldly conformity! I find that the people of God today are largely a prayerless people. They are largely a worldly people. They are largely an untaught people. The Bible is neglected; the Throne of Grace is forsaken; the prayer meeting plays an unimportant part in the life of the vast majority of believers. We cannot go out and fight this war until judgment commences in our own hearts. I trust we will all be slain by that Sword so that we can rise up from the place of death to share the resurrection power of Christ and go forward in the battlefield for Him who has called us to be soldiers of the Cross.

Judgment is not enough. There must be the empowering of the Spirit of God.

We are not called to fight at our own charges. We are not called to use our puny little talents against the massive foes who surround us. The battle is the Lord's, and He alone gives the victory. The Spirit of God is the Heavenly Paraclete, the One called alongside to help, and I can call Him in to help me. I trust you will call Him into your life so that the purging, cleansing, sanctifying work might be done, and then, with your life on the altar, empowered and filled with the Spirit of God, you will be able to go forward to victory.

Now, the hand of Othniel prevailed against Chu-shan-rish-a-tha-im and the land had rest forty years. As long as God's man lived, as long as God's man applied the Word of God and showed the example, God gave rest. Then we read these words in verse 11: '*Othniel the son of Kenaz died.*' How often those words have been written in the history of the Christian Church. 'John Calvin, God's servant, died, and then apostasy set in in Geneva. John Knox, God's servant, died, and then apostasy set in in Scotland. Archbishop Cranmer, Bishop Latimer and Bishop Ridley died, and then apostasy set in in England. As long as God's man, preaching God's truth, leads the people of God in the ways of God, there is rest, but when he dies, his ministry is forgotten. You can go to the great Churches of our land where men of God once stood, and as long as they stood those Churches were kept firm on the rock-solid for God. They were granite-like in their stand, and as the waves of apostasy dashed themselves unrelentingly at their base they stood unmoveable, unchallengeable, impregnable and incorruptible, but when God's man died the Church left the path of truth, and sin again entered in amongst them.

The Resistant Judge

Chapter 3:12: '*And the children of Israel did evil again in the sight of the Lord*', and then you read this: '*The Lord strengthened*

Eglon the king of Moab against Israel because they had done evil in the sight of the Lord.'

The Lord strengthened the IRA against the people. That is a startling thought, is it not? Why God permits evil men to be strong! Why God permits evil men to do wrong! Why God permits the ascendancy and dominance of evil in the land! It is a sovereign God who does it.

A Trinity of Evil

God strengthened Eglon the King of Moab. We have a trinity here - we have Moab, Ammon and Amalek.

Moab was the illegitimate child of Lot and one of his daughters. *Ammon* was the other illegitimate child of Lot and his other daughter. *Amalek* was of the children of Esau. Two men who were outside God's will, Lot and Esau. Oh, they came of good stock. The worst enemies of the Christian Church come out of the Christian Church itself.

Here we have a three-fold conspiracy between Moab, Ammon and Amalek. This speaks of the flesh; this speaks or the departure of God's children from God's law. When the people of God depart from the will of God there will always be trouble as a result, and children of trouble will be multiplied.

'The children of Israel cried unto the Lord.' (v.15) That is parallel with verse 9. The way back is the prayer meeting. When the Churches start going back to the Bible they will go back to the prayer meeting.

Some time ago I heard about a Church which was having a rather lean time, so they called their members together to have a church business meeting. (It is not a church business meeting that is needed when the church is filled with dearth and deadness - it is a prayer meeting that is needed. Quit your talking and get on your knees before God!) One man suggested that if they removed every alternate pew they would have more leg-room and their small congregation would look larger. They did this, and then decided to shut off part of the building and make it into an entertainment centre for young people. Do you think that Church survived? No, it got worse, and its latter state was worse than its first.

The way back to God is to cry unto the Lord. I do not think God's people are crying unto the Lord. I do not hear of God's people down on their knees, their eyes filled with tears, saying, Oh, God Almighty, do something! When the Bible-believing churches have prayer meetings packed with men weeping and women crying, then we will be on the way to deliverance. 'They cried unto the Lord.' They did not offer dry prayers. Their prayers were saturated with tears.

What did God do? He raised up a deliverer, a man stamped with the attribute of resistance. He was a strange man. If the denomination had met to vote for a leader they would never have voted for Ehud. Leaders are not voted in. Leaders are raised up of God. They are often rejected, despised and hated by the very people who want leadership. They do not like God's man because he brings, unvarnished, God's message. and it is too hot for them.

Who was this man Ehud? He came of the smallest tribe, the tribe of Benjamin.

Ehud and Paul

Is it not interesting to remember that God's great man in the New Testament, Paul, came from the tribe of Benjamin. There is a direct parallel between Paul and Ehud. Think of all the things that Ehud had and all the things that Paul had, and you will find the parallel between these two men of Benjamin.

Notice something more about Ehud. He was not right-handed. He was left-handed. If you look at the margin you will find that he was 'shut of his right hand'. He had no alternative but to use his left hand.

If you had been looking in that day for someone to deliver the people of God you would not have gone for a person who physically was not able to use his right hand, which was needed to grasp the sword. His sword hand was useless. If he had applied for the job the clever fellows would have said, 'Not him. We are sorry, Ehud, but you have not got the use of your right hand. You are no good. You cannot have the job. You are not fit.' God, however, takes the things that are despised, the things that are hated,to bring to nought the things that are.

It was a common thing in this tribe of Benjamin for the people to be left-handed, because we read that the Benjamites were great men with slings and stones, and able to sling a stone with their left hand to a hair's breadth of the target. That is how Goliath was killed. He was a man of war. He was not a fool, and he knew that David had a sling in his hand. Many times in the battle, stones had been slung at Goliath and he had avoided them. Why did he not avoid the stone from the sling of David? Because he was taken utterly by surprise. David had the sling in his left hand, and Goliath was waiting to see him change the sling to his right hand, but before Goliath knew, the sling was above David's head and the stone was on its way. Yes, and as Billy Sunday used to say, 'it hit him between the lamps and put him out for the count with a headache that aspirins couldn't cure.'

Left-handedness

This Book reveals its own mysteries if you study it. There is a lot in the Bible about left-handedness. In fact, there is a lot in the Bible about God's left hand. Oh, I know there is a lot about His right hand, but just study the Book for yourself. I trust I have put you on the scent of something which will do you good and bring you the fragrance of God's power and blessing.

What did Ehud do? He made himself a dagger with two edges. It is not difficult to see the spiritual significance of that sharp two-edged sword which he forged. Chapter 3:16 tells us *'it was of a cubit length, and he did gird it under his raiment upon his right thigh."* Instead of putting it on his left thigh and drawing it with his right hand, he put it on his right thigh so that he could draw it with his left hand. That is exactly how he deceived Eglon. Eglon was waiting to see Ehud's right hand draw a weapon when he rose out of the seat, but he drew it with his left hand. It was all part of the overruling providence of God.

I have read many sermons on this passage of Scripture and those who preached them have very strong words of condemnation for this man. I do not make any condemnation. There will be a lot of preachers who, when they get to heaven, will spend the first millennium apologising to some of the men of the Bible for the hard things which they said about them. I have nothing to say about this man. His service stands and falls to his own master. He did the job God wanted him to do. His methods were strange, and every man who does anything for God will adopt the strangest methods and will be greatly criticised and hammered by the Church of his day. Like Ehud, he will not be a conformist. He will be a non-conformist.

Ehud went in and said to the King, 'I have a message from God for you.'

What is God's message? God's message is the sword of the Spirit, which is the Word of God. Ehud plunged his dagger into the belly of Eglon. Now, Eglon was very fat. Why did the Bible tell us he was very fat? Because Ammon, Moab and Amalek are types of the flesh. That is why we are told he was very fat. This whole picture is a type of the flesh. The sword did the job. Ehud locked the door on a good job and threw away the key and escaped. He then blew a trumpet and called all Israel together.

At the beginning of Judges all Israel responds to the call, but at the end no one responds to the call. Samson was taken by the men of Judah and handed over to the Philistines. So there is a deterioration in numbers answering the call. The remnant testimony becomes smaller and smaller as we come to the end of the Book. Yes, and as we get to the end of this age of grace the remnant testimony for God will become smaller and smaller, the Church will be squeezed, the people of God will only be a remnant, but thank God if they are God's remnant they will win the victory. Under Ehud, the land had rest eighty years, forty years of rest and then eighty years of rest. The rest which Ehud obtained for them was double the rest which they had under Othniel. I believe that rest which they enjoyed under Ehud continued after he had died, so wonderful was the deliverance.

The Persistent Judge

The last man is Shamgar, He is mentioned in chapter 5:6, in the Song of Deborah. *'In the days of Shamgar the son of Anath, in the days of Jael, the highways were unoccupied, and the travellers walked through byways.'*

If anybody had been looking for a victorious Captain, a victorious General, a man of valour, a man of war to fight the Philistines, he would surely have looked for a man skilled with the sword, a man who was a man of war from his youth, and a man who was known for his skill with military weapons. God did not choose such a man. God chose a ploughman. The soldiers of God are essentially ploughmen. They are mainly concerned with the harvest. They battle to make a way for God's plough, and this is where several fundamentalist-separatist Churches in many countries have lost out. They have made their battle the end instead of the means to the end. The end is the preaching of the gospel. The end is the salvation of souls. The end is the building of the Church. The end is the putting in of the plough, the preparation of the soil, the sowing of the seed, and the harvesting of the grain. Alas, many contenders do nothing but contend. They do not sow the seed. When they see dearth in their own churches and no souls being saved they turn upon those who are engaged in evangelism and deride their separatist stand. They condemn their doctrinal stand; they call and label them with names of condemnation. How sad it is that the fundamentalist cause has been torn through petty jealousies simply because contenders did not realise that their contention was a means to the end and not the end itself. Of course I will battle for the faith. Of course I will slay the Philistines. Of course I will give no quarter to the Lord's enemies, but what am I fighting for? I am fighting so that I might put in the good old gospel plough. I am fighting so that I might sow the seed of the everlasting gospel. I am fighting so that I can win men and women for Jesus Christ and build the Church which is His body, the fulness of Him that filleth all in all.

This man Shamgar was a ploughman. He had only one weapon, the ox goad. The ox goad was a staff with an iron spear, or goad, at its end so that it could pierce the ox and goad it on to do the work of ploughing. Who would have chosen such a man to be a General of a victorious army? God chose him. He tried out that weapon. Oh, he had tried it out on the oxen many times, but he thought he would try it out on the Philistines, so he took it and split the skull of one of the Philistines and it did a good job, and he kept on at it. He persisted in doing it, and at the end of the battle six hundred men were slain. Why six? because six is the number of man. The Holy Spirit has all His numbers right. Goliath of Gath had six pieces of armour. Here we have the number of the Antichrist. When I get to heaven I want to converse with Shamgar. I would like him around today, because there are a few apostate skulls which need to be cracked and a few apostate craniums which need to be broken. This wild herdsman, this ploughman for God, became God's man. He was God's laugh at the establishment. God laughs at the establishment and raises up whom He will to do His work.

So we have a consistent judge in Othniel, a resistant judge in Ehud and a persistent judge in Shamgar. May God give us these characteristics in our Christian work, and may this preacher and pulpit be characterised by consistence, resistance and persistence.

'*Whatsoever thy hand findeth to do, do it with thy might.*' Ecc.9:10.

4

DEBORAH'S SONG

Turn to the fifth chapter of the Book of Judges. The Book of Judges is a Book which records sin, sin in all its dark and hideous hue. It chronicles stories of the utmost shame. What shameful things result from sowing the seeds of sin! The Book also casts a dark shadow over the tribes of Israel and over particular families belonging to those tribes. Although Judges is a Book of sin and shame and shadows, it is also a book which contains this wonderful song, for true to His Word, God gives songs in the night. No matter how dark the age may be, in the great purpose and plan of God there is always time for singing and there is always motivation and prompting for song.

As a song this fifth chapter of Judges is majestic. As a doxology it is sublime. As poetry it is dynamic and as history it is most emphatic. But as Scripture, it enshrines great eternal truths. Truth is undateable and truth is always undated. As the principles of truth are true to all ages, so the principles of this song are as applicable today as they were when it was first sung on the banks of the River Kishon by the victorious armies of Israel, led by Deborah the prophetess and Barak the son of Abinoam the judge.

I want you to notice seven great things concerning this song.

(i) The setting of the song. Every song is prompted by its setting. It originates in certain circumstances which so stir the heart of the writer that the song becomes the child of those particular circumstances.

(ii) The subject of the song;

(iii) The start of the song;

(iv) The sorrow of the song;

(v) The soldiers of the song;

(vi) The shame of the song;

(vii) The secret of the song.

The setting of the song

Judges chapter 4:2 gives us the setting of the song. *'And the Lord sold them into the hand of Jabin king of Canaan, that reigned in Hazor; the captain of whose host was Sisera, which dwelt in Harosheth of the Gentiles. And the children of Israel cried unto the Lord: for he had nine hundred chariots of iron; and twenty years he mightily oppressed the children of Israel.'* Because of Israel's sins. Jabin the king of Canaan who reigned at Hazor had afflicted and conquered all Israel, and for twenty long years, with his nine hundred chariots he had mightily oppressed the people of God, so that they were an imprisoned people, a subdued people, a people back in slavery like the slavery of

Egypt, a people who knew nothing of liberty, emancipation or victory. Their soul was downtrodden. They were downtrodden morally and spiritually, and mightily oppressed. From the heart of that oppressed people there was squeezed out a cry, a cry of souls in anguish, a cry of souls in deep trouble, a cry of souls that could no longer bear the burden and affliction that was laid upon them.

Until our Province cries unto the Lord like that, there will be no deliverance. I do not see as yet among God's people the tremendous crying of men and women unto the Lord. I do not hear the sobs of the saints. I do not see the tears on the faces of the redeemed, concerning the bloodshed and darkness and anarchy that has come upon our Province. When God's people are flocking to the prayer meetings, when they are giving up their time on the Sabbath to seek God with all their heart and soul and mind, then deliverance will come swiftly. I trust that God will stir our hearts to cry unto the Lord, that we will come to God's House and cry unto the Lord.

The setting of the song was the setting of a people in anguish, burdened, troubled, afflicted and oppressed by the enemies of God.

The subject of the song

Let us look at some of these Bible songs. Exodus 15:1, *'Then sang Moses and the children of Israel this song unto the Lord, and spake, saying, I will sing unto the Lord, for He hath triumphed gloriously: the horse and his rider hath He thrown into the se. The Lord is my strength and song, and He is become my salvation: He is my God, and I will prepare Him an habitation; my father's God, and I will exalt Him. The Lord is a man of war: the Lord is His Name.'* This is, of course, the song which Moses sang after the

Egyptians were drowned in the Red Sea. The subject is the Sovereignty of God, an all powerful God in Heaven, God's almightiness, God's omnipotence, God's sovereignty.

Before he died, Moses the man of God joined in another song. You will find it in the Book of Deuteronomy chapter 31:30, *'And Moses spake in the ears of all the congregation of Israel the words of this song, until they were ended.'* Notice the theme of this song, *'Give ear, O ye heavens, and I will speak; and hear, O earth, the words of my mouth......Because I will publish the name of the Lord: ascribe ye greatness unto our God,'* - The sovereignty of God, the greatness of God. *'He is the Rock, His work is perfect; for all His ways are judgment,'* - the sovereignty of God. *'A God of truth and without iniquity, just and right is He,'* - the sovereignty of God.

The first song of Moses emphasised God's sovereignty. The last song of Moses emphasises God's sovereignty.

In the Book of Samuel we have one of the great songs of David as he came to the end of his journey. Turn to 2 Samuel 22:1, *'And David spake unto the Lord the words of this song in the day that the Lord had delivered him out of the hand of all his enemies, and out of the hand of Saul. And he said, The Lord is my rock, and my fortress, and my deliverer. The God of my rock: in Him will I trust: He is my shield, and the horn of my salvation, my high tower, my refuge, my saviour; Thou savest me from violence.'* What is the theme? The sovereignty of God, the almightiness of God.

What is true of the Old Testament songs is equally true of the New Testament songs. The song of Zacharias in Luke chapter 1:68-74, *'Blessed be the Lord God if Israel: for He hath visited and redeemed His people. And hath raised up an horn of salvation for us in the house of His servant David.'* That He would grant unto us that we being delivered out of the hand of our enemies* *might serve the Lord without fear.'* Notice the words ' a horn of salvation' - the sovereignty of God. The great theme of that song is the sovereignty of God.

Turn back in that same chapter and you will find the song of Mary, verse 46, *'And Mary said, My soul doth magnify the Lord, and my spirit hath rejoiced in God my Saviour. For He hath regarded the low estate of His handmaiden: for, behold, from henceforth all generations shall call me blessed. For He that is mighty hath done to me great things: and holy is His name,* - the sovereignty of God. Look at verse 52, *'He hath put down the mighty from their seats, and exalted them of low degree',* - the sovereignty of God. God is sovereign, He is almighty, He is omnipotent, He does what He wills in the armies of heaven and among the sons of men, and none can stay His hand or say to Him, 'What doest Thou?' The universal theme of every song in the Bible is the sovereignty of God.

What is the last song recorded in the Bible? It is the new song. You will find it in Revelation chapter 5:9,10, *'And they sung a new song, saying, Thou art worthy to take the book, and to open the seals thereof: for Thou wast slain, and hast redeemed us to God by Thy blood out of every kindred, and tongue, and people, and nation: And hast made us unto our God kings and priests: and we shall reign on the earth.'* There is the sovereignty of God. So in heaven it is the same theme, the sovereignty of almighty God. This was the great truth that put iron and steel into the resistance of our covenanting forefathers. This was the great theme that carried forward the glorious Reformation of the 16th Century. This was the great theme that pervaded the preaching of the Apostles, that God is on the Throne. The Devil cannot win. Sin will not finally triumph. God's truth stands for evermore. Heaven and earth may pass away, but the Word of the sovereign God of heaven shall never pass away.

If you look at this song of Deborah, it is filled with the sovereignty of God.

Verse 2, *'God is a God of vengeance'* - a sovereign God.

Verse 3, *'God is a marching God'* - a sovereign God.

Verses 4 & 5, *' God is a majestic God'* - a sovereign God.

Verse 13, *'God is an omnipotent God'* - a sovereign God.

Verse 14, *' God is an all-controlling God'* - a sovereign God.

Verse 15, *'God is an all-destroying God'* - a sovereign God.

Verse 16, *'God is an all-gracious God'* - a sovereign God.

So there is one subject to this song. It is the sovereignty of God. As I look away from the terrible confusion that is in this world today, and look away from all the sorrows and the sins and the shame and the shadows of this earth, I go beyond the stars and beyond all the solar systems, I go away to that place above all heavens where the everlasting God the Lord sits in omnipotent majesty and power, and I say today from a heart that has God's peace, *'The Lord God omnipotent reigneth, and He shall reign until every enemy licks the dust at His feet.'*

Brethren and sisters in Christ, we are going to win, for we are on the winning side! That should start a song in your heart today. No matter what enemy comes, whether it be the enemy of disease or sickness, the enemy of depression or oppression, the enemy of death, the enemy of the grave, the enemy of the shroud and the coffin, the enemy of loneliness, desertion, desolation or destitution, it matters not, praise God, God will win the war, God will get to Himself the victory. God is upon the Throne. That is the subject of this song.

The start of the song

Let us look at the start of the song, and this is very important. Where does it start? Verse 3, *'Hear, O ye kings, give ear, O ye princes, I even I will sing unto the Lord, I will sing praise to the Lord God of Israel, Lord when Thou wentest out of Seir, when Thou marchest out of the field of Edom.'* Why does it start with Edom? Why does it start with Mount Seir? Edom was, of course, Esau. Mount Seir was the possession of Esau. But Esau was not the chosen of the Lord. I will tell you where the song starts. It starts in God Almighty's sovereign choice of His people. *'Jacob have I loved, Esau have I hated.' 'Ye have not chosen Me, but I have chosen you'.* We are now in the mystery of foreordination, that all things are ordered by God in His sovereign will, and we are now in the mystery of Divine election, that *'whom He did foreknow, He also did predestinate.'* We are now in the mystery of eternity, and that is where the song starts. 'Before the hills in order stood, or earth received her frame', away in eternity, that is where the song had its origin. It was born in eternity, and praise God it is going to be sung to all eternity. It had its origin in the very Throne of God Himself.

But there is something more. Edom is represented in scripture as a type of Mount Calvary. Turn to Isaiah 63. (Isaiah 53 and Isaiah 63 should always be read together, because they are parallel passages). *'Who is this that cometh from Edom, with dyed garments from Bozrah? this that is glorious in His apparel, travelling in the greatness of His strength? I that speak in right-eousness, mighty to save.'* I want you to notice the unity of scripture. My song tells me that the Lord marched out of the field of Edom. Isaiah 63 says *'He travels in the greatness of His strength.'* Notice the unity of the Book. Edom, a type of Calvary - *'Who is this that cometh from Edom, with dyed garments from Bozrah?'* Why do I sing this morning? I sing not only because of the eternal choice, I sing because of the eternal Cross.

At the Cross, at the Cross
Where I first saw the light,
And the burden of my heart rolled away,
It was there by faith I received my sight,
And now I am happy all the day.

That is where I learned the song, when I came to Jesus and found in Him my all in all.

Perhaps there is some burdened soul and your heart is filled with sadness. Oh, come to the Cross today, come to the Saviour. He will lift your burdens, wash away your sins. Come today, for there is room at the Cross for you.

Yes, the song starts in eternity, it starts at the Cross.

The sorrow of the song

Look at the sorrow of the song. Ah, this song strikes a plaintive note. In verse 6 it talks to me about desolation, *'When the highways were unoccupied and the travellers walked through byways.'* It tells me of desertion, *'They chose new gods: then was war in the gates: was there a shield or spear seen among forty thousand in Israel?'* There is sorrow in this song. The days of blessing have departed and the days of shame, compromise and declension have come in. The days when Deborah were the days when there were new gods; days when men had turned away from the true Jehovah and set up shrines of idols among the groves and hills of the pleasant promised land. Such is our day. It is a day of new religions, new gospels, new Bibles, new theologies, new ecclesiastical politics. There is a craving like the craving of the Athenians for some new thing.

I was reading in the Library of the House of Commons this week that the Archbishop elect of Canterbury has received eulogy and praise from the official organ of the homosexuals in England, and they claim that the new Archbishop elect of Canterbury is most favourable to homosexuality and that he has ordained many practising homosexual clergymen in the church. They believe the consecration of the new Archbishop will lead to the liberation of the homosexuals in the Church of England. How are the mighty fallen, and the weapons of war perished! It is an evil day!

There is a plaintive note in this song. It talks about the highways forsaken, of the byways chosen rather than God's great highway. Is that not a parallel to our day?

The soldiers of the song

Look at verse 9, and here we find the singers of this song, Deborah and Barak. This was a duet. The first song recorded in the Bible was also a duet. It was sung by Moses and the children of Israel after the Red Sea crossing. The last song recorded in the Bible is a duet, the song of Moses and of the Lamb. You will remember that there were two preachers in prison in Philippi and they sang a duet. It caused an earth-quake , yes, but it also caused a revival. The duets in the Bible are worthy of study.

In verse 9 of Judges 5 the hearts of the singers were towards the governors of Israel, the elected leaders of the people, those who were in places of authority. What did they do? They *'offered themselves willingly among the people. Bless ye the Lord.'* It is always a sad thing when the leaders in God's work hold back in the day of battle. It is always a tragedy in the Church of Jesus Christ when the elected leadership is not in the van when the enemy is to be attacked, when sin is to be challenged and when the Devil has to be confronted.

In this day, however, the governors of Israel willingly offered themselves. They willingly made the sacrifice which was necessary. There was no holding back, no counting the cost. They said, 'Here we are, Deborah, here we are, Barak, here we are, Lord God of Israel. We will make the sacrifice which is necessary. We will make it willingly and joyfully. We will make it with all our hearts and all our souls and all our minds.' These are the soldiers of this song.

God is looking today for people who will make such a willing offering of themselves unto the Lord. How does God feel about the lack of love in the hearts of His people towards Him? How does Christ feel as He looks down into our hearts today? Over the past years there has been so much for the world, so much for the flesh, so much for self, so much for the things of time. How much has there been for God and for God alone? If you are honest you will have to confess that only a tiny fraction has been for God, and the greater part of our lives has been lived for business, for pleasure, for home, for comfort, and for self. God could not write a song about our lives, could He? God is challenging us as a people to make a willing offering of ourselves. These people offered not their prosperity, not the riches of others, but they willingly offered themselves among the people. Oh, that among us there might be a group of dedicated Christian men and women who will give themselves willingly to this task of bringing revival to our land. Oh that we might give ourselves willingly to the holy occupation of intercession and supplication. Wanted! Men and women who will, on their knees, shake the gates of Hell. Where are we going to find such men and women? God is looking for a man to make up the hedge, to stand in the gap. Will all His looking be in vain? It was not in vain in the days of Deborah and Barak.

The end of verse 9 is *'Bless ye the Lord.'* Hallelujah! here is a man, here is a woman who is going to stand for God. Well may the Church shout Hallelujah! when its people willingly give themselves to the Lord.

In verses 14 and 15 of this fifth chapter you will find that God records for all time the people who made the sacrifice. *'Out of Ephraim.'* Who was Ephraim? He was the younger son of Joseph. Joseph's tribe was divided between Manasseh and Ephraim - Ephraim the younger, Manasseh the elder. There was a special blessing given to Ephraim. He was specially blessed as the younger son of Joseph.

'Out of Ephraim was there a root against Amalek.' Who was Amalek? Amalek was that section of the Edomites of whom God said He would war with from generation to generation. Amalek is a type of the Devil and all his works. Now all Ephraim did not come out and fight with Amalek. The entire Church will never rally in this battle against apostasy. It will always be a remnant which will do the fighting. Down through history it was only a tiny minority which went into battle. The Puritans were a minority. The Reformers were a minority. The Covenanters were a minority. The leaders of the great evangelical awakening under Whitefield were a minority. Look at the Book, what does it say? It says 'a root', just a root, but the root sticks in the ground, does it not? The root will not be moved about with the wind. The root will not be subject to breaking up in pieces. It will remain firm. God give us men who will stand firm in this evil day!

The next decade will see in the Churches the greatest apostasy which has ever been witnessed. Is there going to be a root out of Ephraim to stand against Amalek? Is there going to be some man who will put his roots down into the solid Rock of Ages? Is there going to be some woman who is going to say, 'By God's grace I am going to be God's woman, a mother in Israel in this my day? God is issuing a challenge to us all. Are you going to be a root to face the power of Amalek?

Look at the next person, Benjamin. Who was he? He was the youngest son, and yet he was prepared to take his stand. Then of Zebulun it is said, *'they that handle the pen of the writer.'* I was most interested in that statement. When I looked it up in the original I found that it is not to do with writing books, but rather with numbering and making a note of recruits. Zebulun kept the muster role of the army. The pen of a ready writer wrote down the names of those who were going to battle on the side of Deborah and Barak against the enemy, Sisera. From Zebulun came the men who took down the names, who recorded the numbers.

You will remember in Bunyan's Pilgrim's Progress, when Christian came to the House of the Interpreter there was a great battle going on at the gate to the Palace. He saw a man coming forward who said, 'Put down my name.' They put down his name and gave him a sword. He battled against the enemy at the gate. He was wounded and his body streamed with blood, but eventually he fought his way in and was crowned victorious. Have you said to God, 'Put down my name'? Is there some member of the tribe of Zebulun who is going to handle the pen of a ready writer?

Then let us look at the princes of Issachar. They also joined in the battle They were listed among those who stood for God. Notice that there are not many tribes mentioned. All the tribes did not report for the battle, but God specially mentioned those who did. Anything you ever do for God, God will write it up in His Book, and He will have it in everlasting remembrance.

The shame of the song

There were tribes here who brought dishonour to God. Look at the first tribe of them all, Reuben, Jacob's firstborn son. In verse 15 there was division in Reuben and great thoughts of heart. If you look in the margin it reads *'great impressions of heart'*. There was division in Reuben, they did not know what to do. *'Unstable as water, thou shalt not excel* , said Jacob to Reuben on his deathbed. Reuben was a divided tribe and at the end of the day the compromisers won. How often in the Church the compromisers win! How often in the denomination the compromisers win! That is why when you see a compromiser you should run him out the door. Do not give him house room, because he will have a leavening effect on God's people. Anybody who suggests you should pull down the standard, scabbard the sword and just carry on like an ordinary church, is a compromiser. Do not let him live among the people of God, because he will destroy them. Compromise is a deadly poison.

What happened to Reuben? He began to discuss the situation. Dedication to Christ is not for discussion, it is for action. When you get people discussing dedication then they are already sold out. I do not need to discuss anything. God has asked me to give myself to Him and it is not a time for argument. It is a time for commitment. It is a time for sacrifice. What happened? They stayed where they were. They listened to the bleating of the sheep. They abode among the sheepfolds. They put business first.

Is that what you are doing? Are you putting business first? The bleating of the sheep! Is the jingle of the money in the till more important to you than the prosperity of God's work, God's Church and God's people? Room for business,

believer, but no room for Jesus! How much room are you
going to have this week for the prayer meeting?

An old preacher once said, 'You will know the popularity of the denomination by the attendance at the morning
worship service. You will know the popularity of the preacher
if you come to the evening service. But you will know the
popularity of God if you come to the prayer meeting.' That
preacher was hitting the bull's eye!

How popular is God with us? Reuben gave place to
business. He had time for business but no time to fight.

'Gilead abode beyond Jordan', verse 17. Some of the greatest warriors of the Book came from Gilead's mountain. Here,
alas, we have Gilead holding back. The Church which once
fought for God does not always fight for God. Some of the
great historic denominations are not battling for the Lord today. What histories they have, and what battles for the Lord
they fought, but they are not battling for the Lord today. For
them the fight is over, the battle is past. Gilead abode beyond
Jordan, Dan remained in ships. Ashur continued on the
seashore. They kept at their business. 'Let's go fishing. We
are in the fishing business.' They were engaged in a cod war
while there was another war in which they should have been
battling.

How different were the men of Zebulun and Naphtali.
Verse 18, *'They were a people that jeoparded their lives unto the
death in the high places of the field......they took no gain of money.'*
They were not in it for filthy lucre. They were not in it for a
big name. Some people are in controversy for their own
personal egotism and aggrandisement, and that is why they
fight God's children.

Many years ago I made a decision and I have tried to
keep to it. I will not train my guns upon my brethren, but I

will train my guns on the Devil's crowd. There are some people and when you read their literature all they are interested in is doing down God's people. That is all they care about, tearing the heart out of the testimony of some other man of God with whom they do not agree. I am going to keep my guns on the Devil and on the Pope and on the Ecumenists. If people put themselves in the line of fire, that is their fault, not mine. May the Lord save us from turning our swords upon His people and help us to stand true for the Lord.

Zebulun and Naphtali jeopardised their lives. They were not in it for money or personal aggrandisement. In the margin there is a wonderful exposition of 'jeoparded'. It is 'they exposed themselves to reproach'. Ah, if you are going to stand for God you will expose yourself to reproach. The reproaches of those that reproached Christ will fall upon you. This is not a Sunday school picnic. This is a battle to the death in which we are engaged. I wonder are you going to be among the soldiers of the song or are you going to be part of the shame of that song?

The secret of the song

Last of all, we find the secret of the song. Verse 11. *'They that are delivered from the noise of archers in the places of drawing water, there shall they rehearse the righteous acts of the Lord, even the righteous acts towards the inhabitants of his villages in Israel: then shall the people of the Lord go down to the gates.'*

There are five things here.

(i) Service for Christ expounded - *'the places of drawing water.'*

Let me give you a hint. If you study Genesis 26 you will find that Isaac was a man who re-dug the wells which his father Abraham had dug, but which had been blocked up by the Philistines. We have to get the drawing water flowing again.

Four wells are mentioned - Esek, Sitnah, Rehoboth and Sheba. They mean contention, hatred, the oath, and room. If you re-dig the wells there will be contention. God will, however, be faithful to His oath, and He will make room for
• the man who draws the water from the wells of salvation.

(ii) Opposition to Christ explained - '*the noise of archers.*'

Joseph was a tree planted by the well, whose branches ran over the wall, and the archers shot at him. There will be opposition. Never be afraid of opposition. You need to be afraid of no opposition. When I receive threatening letters I thank God. When I do not receive them I am afraid, because if a man is really going to murder you he does not send you a threatening letter. So never be afraid of opposition. We hear the noise of the archers, the Pope on the battlements of the Vatican with his archer's bow and his quiver firing his poison arrows across the world. The Pope is going to have more trouble, for if you read Revelation 17 the beast is going to use his horns to make the woman desolate. The Word of God will be fulfilled, and Rome is going to be torn asunder from within and not from without. That is what the Book says and the Book is right. I am glad I have got this blessed Word.

(iii) Deliverance by Christ experienced - '*they that are delivered.*'

Thank God there is deliverance for the people of God. The Lord is going to deliver us. (iv) Acts of God expressed - '*the righteous acts of the Lord.*'

Then we have, last of all and best of all,

(v) Victory through Christ expected - '*We will go down to the gates.*'

What were the gates? They were the place of the council. *'I will build my church, and the gates of hell shall not prevail against it.'*

I will go down to the gates armed with the name of the Lord Jesus Christ and the Blood of the Lamb.

Are you going to give yourself to God to-day? Are you going to put your life on the altar, believer? Are you going to be God's man? Are you going to be among Zebulun? Are you going to be among Reuben? Are you going to be among the tribe of Dan or among the tribe of Ephraim? Choose your tribe today!

5

GIDEON -
HIS CHARACTERISTICS

'And the Lord looked upon him and said, Go in this thy might, and thou shalt save Israel from the hand of the Midianites: have not I sent thee?' Judges 6:14.

Just a little aside - In 1970 I had a challenge, the challenge as to whether or not I should respond to the people of North Antrim and fight the North Antrim seat for the Westminster Parliament. Humanly speaking, it was a crazy thing to consider, because the Official Unionist majority was something in the region of 26,000. Some of my friends told me it was foolish to consider it, but God impressed this very verse upon my heart, and there was no escape from it. I announced to my congregation that I was going to fight the seat and that I was going to win it. Again, some people expressed grave doubts, but I had not a doubt about it, and the majority was turned into a majority for me.

It was the biggest turnover ever recorded in British electoral history, and is in the Guinness Book of Records. So this text is very precious to me.

This text divides itself easily into three parts.

(i)   The commission announced - 'Go.'

(ii) The courage assured - 'in this thy might, have not I sent thee?'

(iii) The conquest affirmed - 'thou shalt save Israel from the hand of the Midianites.'

(i) The commission announced - 'Go.'

God is a God of action, and all through the Bible we find the Go of God, the commission of God to his people to go and fulfil His commands.

It is important that every believer realises and recognises that God wants them to obey the 'go' of the great commission.   There is not one word in the Bible about the Church crying to sinners to come and hear the gospel, yet all the machinery of the Church today is organised on the basis that sinners should come to Church.   That is not God's method. God's method is that the Church should go to sinners, and if the Church is not going to sinners the sinners will not be going to the Church.   The great commission is to go.   Many Churches today are entertaining the goats and not feeding the sheep.   The purpose of the Church is not to entertain the goats, the purpose of the Church is to feed the sheep with the gospel of Jesus Christ.

Gideon was told to go.   He was not told to wait until the Midianites attacked him.   He was told to go and take the offensive and attack the Midianites.   Would to God the Church of Jesus Christ to-day, embattled though it is, would come off the defensive and go on the offensive for the Lord Jesus Christ. It is a shame when false cults go on the offensive and the Church is on the defensive. May God help us to go on the offensive for His name.

(ii) The courage assured - 'in this thy might, have not I sent thee?'

You will notice that the might has a human aspect as well as a divine aspect, because God uses human instruments and wields His omnipotence through human weakness.

Gideon was not naturally a man of courage. In fact he had one great characteristic, he was afraid. He was a man characterised by fear. You will find an illustration of this fear in verse 11, *'Gideon threshed wheat by the winepress, to hide it from the Midianites.'* He carried on his work in secret. He was not prepared to come out publicly and challenge the invaders, and so he took it to a place of concealment and to a hiding place. In verse 27 we read, *'he feared his father's household, and the men of the city.'* When God sent him down to the encampment of the Midianites He said, *'If thou art afraid to go down.'* Here was a man filled with fear, and yet God gave to him the necessary courage and strength to go and fight the Lord's battles, because the necessary power is God's power, reaching perfection in human weakness.

Gideon was a man who dwelt much upon his own poverty and the lack of his own talents. Look at verse 15, *'My family is poor in Manasseh, and I am the least in my father's house.'* He had no confidence in his own talents, his own ability, his own standing or the strength of his own natural generation. He was a man who had learned that if he were going to be courageous for God, God must inject into him that courage.

Self-reliance and human confidence is all in vain in this battle. We need a courage that is divine. No matter how naturally courageous a man may be, he is absolutely useless and fruitless in the battle against God's enemies. We need a courage which comes from God, a courage which takes away all human fears and lays them to rest. We require a courage which makes us strong because it is based and founded upon God Himself. If we are going to fight the Lord's battles against the enemies of the gospel in our own land, it is this divine courage and not human courage which we need. Gideon had learned that and learned it well.

Gideon a separatist

Gideon was a separatist. He was a man who was known in the city as a man who did not and would not countenance the worship of Baal. In verse 29 that the men of the city knew immediately who had thrown down the altar of Baal. *'They said, Gideon the son of Joash hath done this thing.'* Why did they come so quickly come to the conclusion that the throwing down of Baal's altar was the handiwork of Gideon? Simply because Gideon had not been bowing at that altar. Gideon already had the reputation of being against the worship of Baal. The reason that they jumped so quickly to their conclusion was because Gideon's past testimony was one of separation, and although he had been doing his work in hiding and in fear, he had not compromised his basic principle of separation.

Gideon an historian

Another thing to be noted about Gideon is that his emphasis was upon the Lord. He was a man who re-membered God's dealings in the past. Look at verse 13, *'And*

Gideon said unto him, Oh my Lord, if the Lord be with us, why then is all this befallen us? and where be all his miracles which our fathers told us of, saying, Did not the Lord bring us up from Egypt? but now the Lord hath forsaken us, and delivered us into the hands of the Midianites.' In the Authorised Version when the word 'LORD' is printed in small capitals it is the word 'Jehovah'. Could I draw your attention to the fact that the word 'Jehovah' occurs three times in this verse, and could I make a suggestion that when you are reading the Old Testament you should mark how many texts have 'the LORD' in them three times. Do you wonder why there is that continual repetition of 'the LORD' ? It is because He is a triune God. Underneath the surface of these texts God is establishing His own divine triunity, the triunity of the Godhead, the Lord, the Lord, the Lord.

I believe that God's Church needs to give attention to the history of God's great doings and interventions in the past. God has not finished with His Church. Some people believe that because the age of grace is climaxing (and there is no doubt about that) and the coming of the Lord is drawing very near (and there is no doubt about that), that the church need not expect great movements of God's power. I do not believe that. I believe that when the Lord comes for His Church she will be prepared as a bride adorned for her husband, and I know of nothing which can adorn the Church more than a gracious and blessed outpouring of the Spirit of God. I do not believe that God has finished His mighty works on earth. I believe that God's works are never repeated, that they are always greater still, and I am looking for a mighty demonstration of God's power in the end time. When the enemy shall come in with an end time flood the Spirit of the Lord shall lift up a standard against him. So we can expect great things from God. May God help us to attempt great things for Him!

Gideon a prayer warrior

Not only was Gideon a separatist and an historian, he was also a man of prayer. In fact his whole life is signified by prayer. Here in verse 13 is a prayer and it comes from the depths of his heart. He says, 'O God, Thou dids't mighty things for us in Egypt but now we are forsaken, we are under the heel of the enemy. Why is it that Thou hast forsaken us O God?' This is the anguished cry of an impassioned heart, a man who interceded.

In verse 17 Gideon says, *'If now I have found grace in Thy sight.'* and he makes another petition. At the end of the chapter he makes yet another about the fleece. There is a wonderful little word here which we must not miss in chapter 7:15, *'And it was so, when Gideon heard the telling of the dream, and the interpretation thereof, that he worshipped.'* He did not say, 'It's a good job I am going to win the battle, let's hurry back and start the fight.' He took time to pray. He took time to worship.

The supreme test of a person's spirituality is what they do when trouble hits them. What do you do? Do you immediately pray? The believer who prays immediately trouble comes is a spiritual believer. The believer who seeks help from others when trouble comes is not a spiritual believer. A man is known by the instantaneousness of his prayer life. Here was a man who was in the very midst of the enemy, he had just received good news, but he did not hurry away. He took time to worship. May God help us to take time to be holy, and to speak with our Lord!

Gideon a sacrificer

Notice that Gideon was not only a man of separation, a man of memory and a man of prayer, but he was a man of sacrifice. The oak trees in scripture are all types of the Cross. Where did the angel of God meet Gideon? Look at chapter 6:11, *'He sat under an oak.'* Where did Gideon offer the sacrifice? Verse 19, *'and brought it out unto Him under the oak.'* The oak trees in scripture are very important. Where did God meet Abraham before He destroyed Sodom? Under the oak tree. Where did God deal with Jacob? He buried the idolatrous instruments of his family and the earrings of his children under the oak tree on the way to Bethel. The oak tree is a type of the Cross. Where was Absalom, a type of the flesh, hung by the hair of his head? Upon the oak tree. The oak in scripture is always a type of the Cross.

Gideon was a man of sacrifice. He realised that God only met with His people in the place of sacrifice. There is no place of meeting between man and God but at the Cross. You will not meet God at a baptismal font; you will not meet God savingly at the Lord's Table. The ordinances of the gospel are proper in their own place, but they have no saving light and cannot convey saving grace to the soul. It is flying in the face of God's truth to say that a child is regenerated by infant baptism. It is just as great a lie to say that a grown man or woman is converted to God through baptism by immersion. The only liquid which can wash away sin is the blood of the Lamb. Salvation is by Christ's blood alone.

> Have you been to Jesus for the cleansing power?
> Are you washed in the blood of the Lamb?
> Are you fully trusting in His grace this hour?
> Are you washed in the blood of the Lamb?

That is the great question you need to ask yourself. God only meets men at the Cross.

'I am the way, the truth and the life', said the Lord Jesus, *'no man cometh unto the Father but by Me.'* So you don't come by the Church, you don't come by ritual, you don't come by ceremony, and you don't come by sacrament, you come to God by Jesus alone. If you have not come by Christ you have not come at all.

Gideon had learned that truth. He was a man of the Cross, a man of sacrifice.

Gideon a spiritual man

The next thing you must note is that he was a man of the Spirit. Verse 34, *'But the Spirit of the Lord came upon Gideon, and he blew a trumpet.'* The trumpet in scripture speaks of the sounding forth of God's Word. The Spirit of God is never divorced from the Word of God. If a man tells you he is led of the Spirit to do something which is completely contrary to God's Word, you will know that that man is in error and that he is a liar. The Word of God and the Spirit of God are in absolute agreement, because it was the Spirit of God who wrote the Book. The Spirit of God never never contradicts God's Word. I have little time for people who come to me and say 'I am sure it is the will of God to do a certain thing,' and that thing is clearly condemned in God's Word. There are people who tell me that it is the will of God for them to remain in apostasy, to remain in the World Council of Churches, and to remain in the ecumenical movement. They tell me they can do good work by staying in. I open the Book, and it tells me clearly, *'Have no fellowship with the unfruitful works of darkness, but rather reprove them'*. It tells me *'Come out from among them and be ye separate, and touch not the unclean thing.'* When God says 'Come out' it does not mean 'Stay in.' God means what He says in His Book. *'From such turn away.'*

That is what the Book says about false teachers. The Spirit of God came upon Gideon and he blew the trumpet. The Spirit-ordained ministry will blow the trumpet of God's Word, and it will be a rallying trumpet. It will not be a call to ease or compromise or pleasure. It will be a call to war. How we need to rally the people of God for the battle! May God help us to blow that trumpet in these desperate days in which we live!

Judges chapter 6:34, *'And Abiezer was gathered after him.'* The very people who wanted to kill Gideon were the very people who were the first to come and stand with him. *'When a man's ways please the Lord, He maketh even his enemies to be at peace with him.'* Proverbs 16:7.

Do not be afraid when the world is against you, for God has a people even amongst those who now cry for your blood, but who eventually will stand with you in the battle.

Gideon a faithful man

I have one last word to say about this man. He was a man of faith. I am very happy about Gideon because his faith was like my own, it was very weak. I like the men who are depicted thus in scripture. God does not depict them as supermen, God depicts them as men of like passions as ourselves. Gideon needed a sign. He was always looking for a sign. Now, it would be great if our faith was so strong that we would not need a sign, but alas, our faith needs signs to prop it up and strengthen us. I love when Gideon said, 'Lord I will put the fleece on the floor and if it is wet and the floor is dry I will know that everything is well.' God did this, and Gideon was able to wring the water out of the fleece, but still he was not satisfied. How like ourselves. when God orders us to do something and we are not satisfied. Gideon said,

'Please do not be angry with me' - he knew the Lord should have been angry with him - 'But', he said, 'Let the fleece be dry and the floor wet with the dew.' God did this also.

It is interesting to note that both the signs Gideon asked for were linked to the sacrifice.

The first sign he asked for was after he made the sacrifice. How is a fleece obtained? Only when the lamb is slain. God gives no signs to His people but the signs which come from the Cross. We commence our Christian life at the Cross, and we finish it at the Cross. That is why we need to sing, 'Jesus, keep me near the Cross.'

If you have never been to the Cross, may God bring you to the Cross today and may you trust in Christ and be eternally saved by His atoning blood and finished work on that tree of redemption, for Jesus' sake!

6

FAINT YET PURSUING

I want to link the text 'Faint yet pursuing' with a verse in Judges chapter 7, in which we read *'And they blew the trumpets, and brake the pitchers which were in their hands: and they cried, The sword of the Lord and of Gideon,'* and to discuss five things - (i) the voice of the trumpet; (ii) the vessel of the tactic; (iii) the vision of the torch; (iv) the valour of the tested; (v) the victory of the triumphant.

The Voice of the Trumpet

Let me briefly sketch in for you the historical setting. The Midianites had put their iron heel of tyranny upon the children of Israel. God visited Gideon and prepared him and commissioned him to be the deliverer. Then something happened to Gideon. Chapter 6:34, *'But the Spirit of the Lord came upon Gideon, and he blew a trumpet; and Abiezer was gathered after him. And he sent messengers throughout all Manasseh; who also was gathered after him: and he sent messengers unto Asher, and unto Zebulun, and unto Naphtali; and they came up to meet them.'* You will notice that the voice of the trumpet was inspired by the power of the infilling of the Spirit of God.

The Bible is full of trumpets and the voice of trumpets. Could I remind you that the whole dispensation of God's grace is going to end with the voice of the great trumpet. *'For the trumpet shall sound, and the dead in Christ shall rise first, and we shall all be changed, in a moment, in the twinkling of an eye, at the last trump.'* There will be no trumpet after the last trumpet. The voice of the trumpet is only effective when it is inspired by the Spirit of God.

If you study the Book of Leviticus you will find that there are two silver trumpets mentioned there. They are symbolical. They are typical. They prefigure the gospel. Why two? Because two is the number of witness. *'In the mouth of two or three witnesses every word may be established.'*

The gospel trumpet needs to be sounded today.

Across the world there are faithful men of God who are sounding the gospel trumpet, but the gospel trumpet is ineffectual because it is not being blown by the lips of men who are filled with the Holy Ghost. The great essential today is that we might know the enablement and the enduement of the power of the Spirit of God.

Gideon gathered an enormous crowd of people, but the Lord said 'They are too many.' The Lord had to do a separating work, a segregating work. He had to go in among them and separate them, and of the thousands who came to battle He only took three hundred to do the work. God must get a minority, and He deals and works through minorities. He does not need a whole congregation to be right. If He can get half a dozen people with fire in their souls then there is enough fire to ignite the whole Church.

God did a separating work. He got three hundred men who had steel in their spines. They refused to budge or bend. They were filled with courage, filled with joy, filled with zeal, filled with enthusiasm and filled with strength. Then He said, 'By these three hundred men I will defeat the armies of Midian.'

When Gideon returned after hearing the dream of the man down in the camp of Midian, what did he do? He put a trumpet in every man's hand. The voice of the trumpet! Every man had the same musical instrument given to him.

There is no such thing as a one man ministry in the Church. The ministry of the Church is the ministry of the whole Church. Every believer has a part in this ministry. Only one man can speak at a time, but the whole Church should be blowing a trumpet with the preacher as he blows the trumpet in the pulpit. God has given you a trumpet, believer. Are you blowing it? It is a good thing to blow the trumpet. I trust that there will be born in our hearts a desire to blow the trumpet. Brother, blow the trumpet so loud as to blow the brains out of the Devil and out of the powers of darkness. Oh, that every child of God would say, 'I am going to blow the trumpet. I am going to blow the trumpet of prayer.' Brother, sister, what is wrong with you? Has the Devil so chloroformed you that you cannot awake out of the sleep which has fallen upon you? The world is going to hell. Rise up and blow the trumpet in the name of the Lord Jesus Christ.

It was not a very difficult thing to do, was it, to blow a trumpet? God did not say to them, 'Go and fight the Midianites.' He said, 'Blow the trumpet.' The Word of God does the fighting. It is not the power of man that does the fighting.

The Vessel of the Tactic

Let us look, secondly, at the vessel of the tactic. You see, God showed Gideon the way to do it, and the first thing was that every man's vessel was to be emptied. What was in the vessel? Chapter 7:8 tells us there were victuals in the vessel. These victuals had to be emptied out of the vessel. 'Emptied, that Thou mightest fill me.'

If we are going to blow the trumpet we must first of all be emptied. 2 Tim.2:20,21, *'But in a great house there are not only vessels of gold and of silver, but also fo wood and of earth; and some to honour, and some to dishonour.   If a man therefore purge himself from these.'*   Here is an emptying that I must do. It is not enough to say 'Lord empty me.' You have got to do the emptying yourself . It is not enough for me to say 'Lord empty me' when I am busy filling my heart with both hands. I have to do a purging. You have to do a purging, and if you purge yourself from these *'you will be a vessel unto honour, sanctified, and meet for the master's use, prepared unto every good work.'* (verse 21).

The vessels were then filled with a torch, and if you look in the margin of your Bible, a firebrand was put into every vessel. I want to be a firebrand for God.

An old lady went to John Wesley and said, 'Our preacher is a very poor preacher, Mr. Wesley; he is no good.' Wesley replied, 'Madam, pray that the Lord will set him on fire, and when He does that, the people will come out to see him burn'. You need to pray the preacher on fire. Mr. Spurgeon once said, 'If you have a fireman in the pulpit there will not be any snowmen in the pews.' We need to be filled with the torch of fire.

Now, before the fire lit up the camp of the Midianites it first of all lit up the vessels of the chosen three hundred. Unless I am lit up with the light of God i will never be able to light the world for Jesus Christ. Unless God has lighted us we will never light the world. Our whole being must be filled with light. Oh, to be filled with the fire and light of the Spirit of God! That is what we all need.

The vessel had to be completely destroyed so that the light might shine forth. Unless we are prepared for the utter destruction of the flesh we will not shine. That vessel was an earthen vessel, which speaks of the earthy man - Adam means 'red earth'. He was made of the dust of the earth. God must break us on the Cross so that Christ might increase while we decrease. When we die in Him then we live unto righteousness.

The Vision of the Torch

When the vessels were smashed, the brands of fire lit up the whole camp of the Midianites. What happened? The three hundred men got a vision. They could not see anything until the fire torches burned, and then what did they see? They saw men fleeing. *'Every man stood in his place round the camp, and all the host ran.'* (Judges 7:21).

I tell you, if you get the light of God upon the rebels they will flee. You just need God's light. This is a powerful Book, you know. The Bible brought down the great pagan temples in the first century and the Romish gods in the 16th century, and praise God it can do the same today. May God give us vision, the vision of the torch. They saw men running and crying in fear, and the three hundred blew the trumpets and the Lord set every man's sword against his fellow. God puts confusion on the enemies of the gospel. This is the way to fight God's battle, with the vessel broken, the light shining, the trumpet sounding and men crying out 'The sword of the Lord and of Gideon.'

It is our sword as well, for God has given it into our hands. This is the way to victory, and God wants His Church to have the vision of the torch. God will dispel the enemies. I am not afraid. We are going to win the battle. The Lord is on our side, and better than that, we are on the Lord's side. That is the best thing of all. Hallelujah!

The Value of the Testing

Judges 8:4, *'Faint, yet pursuing them.'*   The great tragedy in God's work is that people are not baptized with stickability. They do not keep at it. The great temptation is to run away, even after there has been a great victory. May the Lord help us to stick at it! Here was Gideon, he was faint, but he had not given up the battle. He wanted to see it through to the end. God's people will have the valour of the tested. Why did God separate these three hundred men? Because He knew that they would go right on to the end of God's road and God's will.

'Though none should join me, still I will follow,
No turning back, no turning back.'

This was the song they sang, and what happened? Oh, there was opposition. The men of Ephraim opposed him. The men of Succoth opposed him. The men of Penuel opposed him. They would not help him. When you are in the stiffest conflict there will be brethren and sisters in Christ who will not help you. They will not come to the help of the Lord against the mighty. You will fight a lonely battle but even though you are faint, keep pursuing, because God is going to give you the victory. You might feel like running away, but don't do it - stick like a limpet to the Rock, covet not the easy road. Only a coward runs away. It is a live fish which swims against the current. God wants us to battle on, faint yet pursuing.

The Victory of the Triumphant

Last of all, there is the victory of the triumphant. Zebah was slain and Zalmunna and Oreb also were slain. All the men who opposed Gideon were slain, yet the day of Gideon's victory was the day of his greatest backsliding. Verse 21, ' *And Gideon arose, and slew Zebah and Zalmunna, and took away the ornaments that were on their camels' necks.'* In the margin it reads 'Ornaments like the moon" because they were moon worshippers, Ishmaelites. Verse 24-27, *'And Gideon said unto them, I would desire a request of you, that ye would give me every man the earrings of his prey. (For they had golden earrings, because they were Ishmaelites). And they answered, We will willingly give them. And they spread a garment, and did cast therein every man the earrings of his prey. And the weight of the golden earrings that he requested was a thousand and seven hundred shekels of gold; beside ornaments, and collars, and purple raiment that was on the kings of Midian, and beside the chains that were about their camels' necks. And Gideon made an ephod thereof, and put it in his city, even in Ophrah: and all Israel went thither awhoring after it: which thing became a snare unto Gideon, and to his house.'* What a sad ending. A man of tremendous blessing who became a party to idolatrous worship.

Did you ever notice that in Genesis chapter 1 God did not call the sun 'the sun'? He called it 'the greater light', and He called the moon 'the lesser light'. The names 'sun' and 'moon' were names given to the greater and lesser lights by idolatrous worshippers. The sun has been the object of worship and adoration for the greater part of the people of the East. It is thought to be the sun which the Venetians worshipped under the name of Baal, the Moabites under the name of Chemosh, the Amorites by the name of Molek and the Israelites by the name Baal, and by the name of the' king of the host of heaven'. They did not separate sun worship from moon worship, which they called Ashtaroth, the queen of heaven.

It is interesting to note the first mention of the sun in the Bible. It is mentioned in its going down. In Genesis 15:12 we read that when the sun went down God spoke to Abraham. The last Book of the Bible tells me about the sun going down forever, when God makes it like black cloth of hair, and the moon turns to blood.

What did Gideon do in the hour of his triumph? He compromised. The end of Gideon's story is a very sad end indeed. It is not the way in which we start which matters, it is the way in which we finish. May God help us not only to start well and continue well, but to complete the race well, for His sake, Amen.

7

THE MAN WHO WOULD NOT GO BACK ON HIS WORD

We now come in our studies to a most interesting and intriguing character, Jephthah. We are not going to spend time on the intervening era which took place between the death of Gideon and the rise of Jephthah. As I pointed out to you when we commenced these studies in the Book of Judges, you will find that there were twelve judges. In fact we have a whole series of twelves in the Bible - twelve patriarchs in the book of Genesis, the twelve sons of Jacob; twelve judges, the twelve apostles, and the twelve tribes of Israel. Twelve is the number of government. The great and final government of the world redeemed and regenerated will be in the City of God, the City which has twelve gates and twelve foundations in which are written the names of the apostles of the Lamb. So the number twelve in scripture is the number of government.

We have in the Book of Judges twelve great men - Othniel, Ehud, Shamgar, Barak, Gideon, Tola, Gaal, Jephthah, Ibzan, Elon, Abdon and Samson. But in all the working of God's plan there will be counterfeits. In reality there are thirteen judges, one of them being the apostate Abimelech. If you care to read the conclusion of the story of Gideon you will find that there rose up in the place of Gideon, his son by a strange woman. This illegitimate son killed all Gideon's true sons except one, and then entered upon a career of destruction and bloodshedding. Abimelech is a type of the Antichrist. The word judge means saviour. Abimelech is a type of the false saviour, the Antichrist in this Book.

The Divine Order

Look at this most intriguing character Jephthah. In Hebrews 11 you find a mention of Jephthah. He is among the heroes of the faith in verse 32. *'And what shall I more say? for the time would fail me to tell of Gideon, and of Barak, and of Samson, and of Jephthah, of David also and Samuel, and of the prophets.'* The numbers in scripture are important. Count them with me: Gideon, one; Barak, two; Samson, three; Jephthah, four; David, five; Samuel, six; and the prophets, seven. Note that these men are not listed in their chronological order. If man had been writing this verse he would have written it historically and chronologically correct. We know that Gideon came after Barak, that Samson came after Jephthah, and that David came after Samuel. Why did the Holy Spirit change the chronological order of these names? Here is the reason for it: in every Biblical seven there is a principle which must be remembered. The fourth of the seven is the central number, and that is the all-important one. The first and the seventh are linked, the second and the sixth are linked, and the third is linked with the fifth. Now work out the principle. Who stands in the centre of this seven? Jephthah. There is a reason why he takes the central place. Think of Gideon, the first in this verse, and then think of the prophets, the seventh in this verse. Who was the first of the great prophets of action? Elijah was the first. What did Gideon and Elijah both do? The first thing Gideon did was to destroy the altar of Baal. What was the great thing which Elijah did on Mount Carmel? He destroyed the altar of Baal. So you see how the first and the seventh are linked.

Then we have Barak, the second, and Samuel, the sixth, linked. What was the great word of Samuel? *'To obey is better than sacrifice, and to hearken than the fat of rams."* What did Barak do? He cursed those that came not to the help of the Lord against the mighty. Oh, they might have been religious in their sacrifices, but to obey is better than sacrifice.

Samson, the third, is linked with David, the fifth. Who were the enemies of Samson? The Philistines. Who were the enemies of David? The Philistines.

In the centre stands Jephthah. Why is Jephthah in the centre? Because he is the personification of a divine principle. Where will you find this principle? In 1 Corinthians 1;29. Is it not wonderful how the Holy Spirit writes His Book? This Book is not man's book. What a mess man would have made if he had tried to write the scriptures! The scriptures dovetail perfectly together, for the Holy Ghost wrote the whole story, knowing the end from the beginning. I Corinthians 1:26, *'For ye see your calling, brethren, how that not many wise men after the flesh, not many mighty, not many noble, are called.'* Here is the principle - *'that no flesh should glory in His presence.'*

Now, who was Jephthah? Had he anything in the flesh of which to glory? No sir! Judges 11:1, *'Now Jephthah the Gileadite was a mighty man of valour, and he was the son of an harlot.'* So he had nothing of which to glory. This brings me to the first great point concerning Jephthah. He had no confidence in the flesh. He could not put his trust in his natural birth or in his heritage.

No confidence in the flesh

There is a great difference between men through birth. Some are born with doors wide open for achievement and attainment. Some are born with every door locked and the chains across every avenue of improvement. Some are born with flowers underfoot, and some are born with thorns underfoot. Some are born sickly and weak in constitution, some are born strong and tough in constitution. Jephthah started life at a great disadvantage. He was looked upon as an intruder, as someone to be driven out, rejected, repudiated and reviled, and in chapter 11 that is exactly what happened to him. Verse 2, *'And Gilead's wife bare him sons; and his wife's sons grew up, and they thrust out Jephthah, and said unto him, Thou shalt not inherit in our father's house; for thou art the son of a strange woman. Then Jephthah fled from his brethren.'* He was driven out; he was a reject; he was unwanted.

How God takes the unwanted things and makes them mighty in His hands as instruments of His omnipotence!

The best types not always with God's man

The second lesson I want you to learn is that those who join themselves to God's people are not always the best type of people. You find that in the life of Jephthah. Chapter 11: 3, *'And there were gathered vain men to Jephthah, and went out with him.'* That has been the story of the church ever since its inception. When the children of Israel went out of Egypt, 'a mixed multitude' went out with them. The Church has never been able to extricate itself from the mixed multitude. It will always be there, and as we face the facts of history we will discover in every great spiritual movement there were those who by their behaviour and conduct and speech brought dishonour to that movement. Nevertheless, God moves in a mysterious way His wonders to perform, and even though Jephthah was surrounded with vain men yet Jephthah was God's man to do God's work in God's way at God's time.

God's selection not popular selection

If you look at verses 4 to 11 you will find that God chooses the leader and God establishes him. God's leaders have never won popular acclaim. They have always been a despised body of men. You remember that Moses went out and thought he would deliver Israel, so he smote the Egyptian who was fighting with an Israelite. The next day he saw two Israelites fighting and he intervened, and one turned round and said, *'Who made thee a judge and a ruler over us? Are you going to kill me as thou didst kill the Egyptian yesterday?'* and Moses fled from the face of Pharaoh. For forty years he was despised, and lived in the backside of the desert, working for his father-in-law, tending his sheep. God was preparing Moses for a great work.

Saul was miraculously saved, but he did not commence his ministry for almost five years after he was converted. Three years he was in Arabia, then he went to Tarsus, his own city, and remained there for at least two years. One would have thought that immediately he was converted he would have started his labours. God said 'No.' God prepares His men. God takes time in preparing His men, and God took time in preparing Saul of Tarsus.

Was it not the same with Joseph? He was despised; he was sold into Egypt; he lay in the prison dungeon and the iron went into his soul, but in God's time he was seen to be God's man at the appropriate time to save the nation.

The same could be said of Caleb and Joshua. They were despised. The children of Israel tried to stone them, but at the end of the day they were God's men to lead the people.

What shall I say of David? David was ostracised, despised and hated. The only people who went to him were those who could not pay their debts. All the debtors went and hid with him in the cave of Adullam. Nevertheless, he was God's man. God chooses His own leader and God establishes His leader in His own providential wisdom. God's leader is not elected by men, God's leader is chosen of God.

The day of adversity reveals the leader

It is in the day of adversity that God's man is revealed. The Gileadites had no time for Jephthah in the day of their prosperity, but when adversity came, when trouble came, when the storm blew, then they sent for Jephthah.

Is it not wonderful how the world has to turn to God's man and God's people when the day of crisis comes. They do not have any time for God's people or God's man before the storm-clouds threaten, but when the storm-cloud bursts then they send for God's man. Chapter 11:7, *'Did not ye hate me, and expel me out of my father's house? and why are ye come unto me now when ye are in distress?'* The day of adversity always throws up God's man. God has a man for the hour, and God has an hour for the man. He never fails!

A student of God's ways and Word

The next point we learn is that God's man is a diligent student of God's ways and God's Word. In verses 12 - 28 of chapter 11 you have the whole history of the children of Israel rehearsed by Jephthah. He knew the history of his people. He had studied the Word and the Works of God. His faith was grounded in the past history of God's dealing with His chosen people. God has dealt mercifully and miraculously with His people in the past. There is no need to be worried today. God is on the Throne and He will see the situation through to the end.

The one thing needful

God's Spirit is the one thing needful. Look at verse 29, *'Then the Spirit of the Lord came upon Jephthah.'* Without the mighty baptism of the Spirit of God all is in vain. *'It is not by might, it is not by power, it is by My Spirit, saith the Lord.'* You can have all the talents, all the ability, you can have everything, humanly speaking, going for you, and you will fail, but if you have God the Holy Ghost and everything else, humanly speaking, going against you, you will still have an abundant and certain victory. We need to be absolutely dependent upon the Spirit of God.

God's man means business

The final lesson is this, that God's man means business. Before he went out to the battle Jephthah made a vow, a solemn vow, a vow that whatever came out and first met him on his return he would offer as a burnt offering unto the

Lord. When he returned from the battle his only daughter was the first to come out to meet him. What did he say? *'I have opened my mouth unto the Lord, and I cannot go back.'* The man who would not break his word! His only child, his daughter, his well beloved, was the price, but he had said, 'I will give her to the Lord' and to the Lord she was given. Now let me say this. He did not offer his daughter as a burnt offering. Such would have been an outrage to the law of God, and God would have condemned such an offering, because the children of Israel were told that they were not to present their children in the fire like the idolaters of Molech.

We need to read this portion very carefully. He could not have God's blessing and offer his daughter as a burnt offering to the Lord. He gave her to a life of entire dedication to God. You have that brought out in verse 39 of this eleventh chapter of Judges, *'And it came to pass at the end of two months that she returned unto her father, who did with her '* - if you have an authorised version of the Bible you will find the word 'according' is in italics, which means that it is not in the original Hebrew - *'to his vow which he had vowed.'* Notice carefully that it does not say 'he did to her according to his vow and offered her up as a burnt sacrifice.'

In the life of Gideon, when he made the ephod God put on record that it was a shame and a curse in the house of Gideon because he had turned to idolatry. If Jephthah had offered his daughter as a burnt sacrifice the Holy Spirit would have condemned it as flying in the face of the direct commandment of God. The key to the text is, *'and she knew no man'* which is the future. It is not 'and she had known no man', but 'she knew no man' (future tense). She remained a virgin in consecration and celibacy all the days of her life.

The next verse brings it out '*that the daughters of Israel went yearly to lament*', and if you

look at the margin you will find that the word 'lament' means 'to talk with her'. So she was still living, and for four days every year the women went and talked with her and rehearsed with her the story of her consecration unto the Lord.

We need to read the scriptures as they are written. We should not draw quick conclusions from a casual reading but draw the conclusion that is written there by the hand of the Spirit.

Jephthah opened his mouth unto the Lord, and he did not go back.

How many of us have opened our mouth unto the Lord in confessing Christ, in identifying ourselves with God's people, in private and public prayer, around the Communion table and in testimony voluntarily, solemnly and deliberately? We have opened our mouth unto the Lord! Let me pose this pertinent question, how many of us have turned back from what we have vowed unto the Lord? To turn back is to insult the Saviour, to prove that we are false, to destroy our happiness and imperil the spiritual life in our souls.

'I have opened my mouth unto the Lord, and I cannot go back.' I trust we will renew our vows before God, and where we have gone back, like Abraham we will return to the place where we made the altar of dedication at the beginning, and that each one of us will be found like Jephthah, perfectly fulfilling our vow to God.

When the Holy Spirit wrote the great eleventh chapter of Hebrews, He put Jephthah right in the central place of the champions, because Jephthah opened his mouth unto God, and he did not go back. May God give us similar dedication of heart and soul this day, for Jesus' sake, Amen.

8

THE HISTORY, TRAGEDY AND MYSTERY OF SAMSON

We come now to study the most interesting of all the judges, the man called Samson. He is the last of the judges in this Book, and he is the twelfth in the series. We will look at his history, his tragedy and his mystery.

Chapter thirteen begins with the conjunction 'and'. You need to remember that there were no chapters in the original scriptures. The only Book divided in the original as we have it today in our Authorised Version was the Book of Psalms. The Psalms were separate songs, but each Book of the Old and New Testaments was written as one undivided narrative. Chapters and verses were made so that a Bible Concordance could be compiled in order that ready reference could be made to particular passages of God's Word. Sometimes chapters divide precious portions and we fail to make the connection, so we must look at chapter twelve to see the connection with chapter thirteen.

Verse 1, ' *And the children of Israel did evil again in the sight of the Lord.*' Notice that the children of Israel, instead of following the Lord and walking with Him and obeying Him, did evil, and here we read that important word 'again'. Mark that word 'again' in your Bible. How true it is in the history of the Church that God gives great deliverances. God sends periods of revival. He sends times of refreshing. He gives gracious outpourings. The Church is quickened, and the walls of Zion are built and the people are singing and rejoicing. Then the tide begins to ebb and the Church languishes, prayer ceases, praises cease, and there is backsliding, corruption and apostasy. It is the history of the Church since the apostolic times right until today. I know no day in the period of the Church so corrupt as the day in which we live.

Abraham Kuyper was a great theologian in Holland. He founded what was known as the Re-Reformed Church, a separatist Church. Just recently the Re-Reformed Church of Kuyper has voted into membership practising homosexuals, and has entered into relationship with the so-called 'gay' society. Think of it! a Church that one hundred years ago was standing where this Church stands today! How did it happen? Because the people do evil in the eyes of the Lord.

The Number Forty

Look at the years in which there was apostasy, forty years. (Judges 13:1). That was the longest period in the reign of the judges. Forty in scripture is the number of probation. The first mention of it was in the days of the flood, when God rained judgment upon the earth for forty days and forty nights. Goliath of Gath challenged Israel for forty days. The Lord Jesus Christ fasted forty days before His temptation. The children of Israel were forty years in the wilderness because of their declension. For forty years the heel of the Philistines was upon the people of God. How dark were those days! How sad were those days! How tragic were those days! It is a terrible thing when apostasy reigns.

One: Samson's Generation

Samson came of the tribe of Dan. In all the tribes of Israel there is no tribe so interesting as Dan. In Revelation chapter 7 you will find the sealing of the tribes. You will also find as you read that chapter that there is no mention of Dan. His name is not called, and there is no one from the tribe of Dan included in the sealing. The family circle is broken. The tribes are eternally fractured. One tribe is not going to turn up in the day when God calls the roll. It is the tribe of Dan.

Dan was the first tribe that went over to idolatry. You will find that in the final chapters of this Book of Judges.

In Genesis 49 there is recorded one of the most interesting scenes in all the scriptures. Old Jacob is dying. He calls his sons around his deathbed. Jacob can see into the future and he says, 'I am going to tell you what shall befall you in the last days.' If you turn to verse 16 you will see the prophecy concerning Samson, *'Dan shall judge his people, as one of the tribes of Israel.'* So when the judges came, one of them was from the tribe of Dan. The scripture was kept, literally, to the last letter, for God's prophetic scriptures cannot be broken.

In the next verse we have the character of Dan, and what a sad character it is. *'Dan shall be a serpent by the way, an adder in the path, that biteth the horse heels, so that his rider shall fall backward.'* The serpent is an accursed creature, cursed from Eden's garden because of the temptation and the fall. Mark what it does. That is the most picturesque description of backsliding in the whole Bible. Here is the Christian riding along the pathway, and suddenly the serpent bites the horse's heels, the horse stops suddenly and the rider falls off backward into the mire and dirt of the highway. Dan was the tribe of the backslider, and Samson is a perfect type of the backslider.

The adder and serpent bit the horse that Samson rode, and how many times he fell backwards into the mire and the dirt. Now, there is a great period of time dividing Jacob and Samson, but the Holy Spirit enabled Jacob to see into the future and to prophecy what lay ahead for the tribes of Israel.

Let us now come back to Judges 13. The name Zorah is an interesting name. It means wasp. Everyone knows that a wasp has a sting. The name Manoah is another interesting name. It means rest. Until we know rest from the sting of the old nature of sin, we will never be able to be champions in the Lord's army. God has to deal with the old nature within us if we are going to know sweet rest in the battle for God. My father used to say, 'You can never fight God's battles unless you have God's peace within your heart.' He was absolutely right.

Knowing

A young man came to me after a service and said, 'I have a battle and I am not winning it. I am being defeated. Is there a path of victory?' I replied, 'Yes, there is a path of victory.' I turned him to Romans 6:6, *'Knowing this, that our old man is crucified with Him, that the body of sin might be destroyed, that henceforth we should not serve sin.'* The first word we need to underline is the word 'knowing'. Jesus said, *'You shall know the truth, and the truth shall make you free.'* The word 'destroyed' does not mean 'annihilated'. It is the same word which is used in Hebrews 2 about the destruction of the Devil. Christ *'destroyed him that hat the power of death, that is to say, the devil.'* The old nature is not annihilated, and neither is the Devil. The old nature and the Devil are, however, rendered powerless at the Cross. I have got to know something. I have got to know that I have died with Christ. If I brought a corpse into the pulpit and praised it, it would not blush. If I criticised it, it would not make any response. If I buffeted it, it would not retaliate. Why? Because it is dead. When you learn that you have died to sin in Jesus Christ, then and only then will you come into the place of victory. There will be no response in your heart to temptation. Why? Because you have died in Christ.

Reckoning

There is another word which we have got to underline, verse 11, 'reckon'. You not only know something, but thank God, you reckon upon it. What does 'reckon' mean? It means that you take your stand upon that truth. I remember hearing Rev. W P Nicholson preach along this line. He put it in his usual inimitable way. He said that after he was saved, the Devil used to come and knock on the door and say, 'Are you there, Billy?' He said, 'I would sit at the fire and say, 'I am not answering him.' The old Devil would knock again, 'Are you there, Billy?' Eventually I would start to argue, and soon I would be down the hall, and open the door, and the Devil had the victory.' He said, 'This happened over and over again until I was miserable. Then one day the Devil came again, knocked the door, but there was no response. Then an old nosey parker who lived next door stuck her nose out of the window and said, 'Did you not hear about Billy? He is dead.'

Mr. Nicholson said, 'When I learned that I had died at the Cross the old Devil had no longer any hold over me.' Mr. Nicholson was right.   You have to reckon yourself dead indeed unto sin, but alive unto God. That is the second word.

Yielding

The third word is 'yielding' - *'but yield yourselves unto God, as those that are alive from the dead.'*   Knowing, reckoning, yielding, that is the way to victory. You want the sting to be dealt with, you want to get to the place of peace? That is the only way. May God help us to remember what the Bible says in that sixth chapter. *'For sin shall not have dominion over you.'* Mark it well! Sin shall not have dominion over you! Glory to God, you can have victory over sin! You can defeat the Devil and the old nature by walking in the path of victory - knowing, reckoning and yielding.

In Judges 13 there are three things underlined in the lesson of Samson's generation.

(i) His birth was special;

(ii) His separation was special;

(iii) His spirituality was special.

In order that he might have a special birth, a special separation and a special spirituality his mother must walk the pathway of separation.

You cannot expect your family to be spiritual if you are not spiritual. You cannot expect your home to be spiritual if you yourself are not spiritual. Parents come to me and mourn the waywardness of their family. When I ask them, 'Do you have a family altar each day? Do you kneel down and pray with your family at some time every day?' they say, 'No, we do not.' Well, how can you expect God's blessing, father, mother,in your generation, if you are not prepared to guide your children's footsteps into the ways of God? You can bend a sapling but you cannot bend an oak tree, and it is only when children are youthful that you can bend them to God's perfect law of submission in obedience to His commandments.

Two: Samson's Education

The second lesson we have got to learn about Samson is found in verses 8 and 12, the lesson of his education. The first lesson is the lesson of his generation. The second lesson is the lesson of his education. Look at verse 8, *'Then Manoah intreated the Lord, and said, O my Lord, let the man of God which Thou didst send come again unto us, and teach us what we shall do unto the child that shall be born.'* Verse 12, *' How shall we order the child, and how shall we do unto him?'* Manoah was prepared to educate Samson in the proper way. He was burdened. He had parental concern. Even before the child was born he was anxious to be spiritually instructed so that he would train the boy up in God's fear, in God's nurture and in God's way.

Oh, that God would put upon Christian parents today the burden of parental responsibility!

Notice in verse 5 that Samson was to begin to deliver Israel out of the hand of the Philistines. It does not say that he was to deliver Israel. He was only to *begin*. Who finished the work that Samson began? None other than King David himself. He started with the slaying of Goliath of Gath and then he slew all Goliath's brothers and eventually dealt with the Philistines. Samson only began the work. *'He shall begin to deliver the children of Israel.'* Although Manoah was a godly man, at times he was foolish. You find his foolishness in verse 22 when he said, *'We shall surely die, because we have seen God.'* Sometimes Christian parents are very foolish too, and say and do foolish things. Manoah's wife said, 'Don't be stupid, man. If God was going to kill us He would not have revealed that He was going to give us a son who was going to begin to deliver Israel.'

The angel of the Lord, the man of God who visited Manoah and his wife was none other than the Lord Jesus Christ Himself. This is one of the great Christophanies, the appearance of Christ in the Old Testament. How do I know that this was Christ? Look at verse 17, '*And Manoah said unto the angel of the Lord, What is thy name, that when thy sayings come to pas we may do thee honour? And the angel of the Lord said unto him, Why askest thou thus after my name, seeing it is secret?*' The word 'is' is in italics, it is not in the original, which reads '*seeing it secret.*' In your marginal Bible you will find the word 'secret' means 'wonderful'. Isaiah says, '*His Name shall be called wonderful.*' This was an appearance of Christ in the Old Testament scriptures.

Remember Samson's generation and his education. Read Numbers chapter 6 and find out what should have happened to Samson's hair. You may never have known about this until now!

9

THE SEPARATION OF SAMSON

In chapter 13 we find that a very strict obligation was placed on Samson's mother. She was to be separated unto God while she carried Samson in her womb. Verse 4, *'Now therefore beware, I pray thee, and drink not wine nor strong drink, and eat not any unclean thing.'* This was a strict role of separation to be followed by Samson's mother. Would to God the mothers of our land today would keep that strict role of separation. What a difference it would make to their children if they were brought up for the Lord.

Christian parents, there is a solemn responsibility laid upon you to obey the commands of God. Your obedience to God's commands will be reflected in your home, in your children and in the blessing of God upon you. God says He will pour out His wrath upon the families that do not call on His name.

Separation the characteristic of Samson

In verse 5 you will find that Samson was to be character-ised by separation. *'For, lo, thou shalt conceive, and hear a son; and no razor shall come on his head: for the child shall be a Nazarite unto God from the womb; and he shall begin to deliver Israel out of the hand of the Philistines.'* The son was to be like his mother. As his mother was not going to drink wine or strong drink nor touch any unclean thing, so her son was not to drink wine or strong drink nor touch any unclean thing. There was something more. He was to take the Nazarite vow from his youth, and it was to be a perpetual vow. He was vowed to the role, the path and the conduct of separation as the result of his birth, and from his birth as the result of the vow.

God's people have had a spiritual birth. It is a birth that is begotten of God by the Holy Spirit. It is a holy birth, and from the day of this birth the believer is bound and chained to a path of separation in obedience to God. There must be nothing of surrender to the world, the flesh and the Devil in the believer's life. He must keep that path of crystal clear, clean-cut separation in obedience to God's law. If he surrenders to the world, if he surrenders to the flesh, if he surrenders to the Devil, then his separation is marred, and immediately the separation is marred the power leaves the believer, the unction of God forsakes him, the Spirit of God departs and the man becomes powerless. He is just as a sounding brass and a tinkling cymbal.

The Law of the Nazarite

In Chapter 6 you will find the law of the Nazarite. We should consider carefully this sixth chapter of Numbers. There is something very important and particular about the vow of the Nazarite. When the vow ceased, when the period of the vow was completed, then the hair which was not to be shaven during the period of the vow, was shaved off in a very special manner. It was only when I began to study afresh the life of Samson that I discovered this very important aspect which reveals the heinousness and dreadfulness of the sin which Samson committed. He allowed himself to be put to sleep on the knees of the harlot. He allowed the hand of a Philistine barber to cut off his locks of separation, and instead of those locks being treated as a holy thing, they were severed from his head, they were trampled under foot by the uncircumcised Philistines as they attacked the now impotent Samson. In Numbers 6:18 you will find that only a holy hand was to be placed on the locks of the Nazarite, and that in the holy place. How unholy are the knees of the harlot Delilah! How unholy was the sacreligious hand of the Philistine barber. *'And the Nazarite shall shave the head of his separation at the door of the tabernacle of the congregation.'* The door of the tabernacle of the congregation was always open. There stood the altar, there stood the laver, and beyond the altar and the laver the Holy Place and the Holiest of All, God's meeting place with His people. That is the place where believers should always stand. The believer should be standing at the place of accessibility to God. He should be standing with the shadow of Calvary upon him. He should be standing with the shadow of the Laver of God's Holy Word and blessed Spirit upon him. He should be standing in the shadow of the Holy Place and in the shadow of the Holiest of All.

Poor Samson! He is in Timnath; he is in the house of a harlot; he is in the place where he is going to lose his power because is is going to lose his separation. What was to be done with the hair of the head of the Nazarite? Numbers 6:18, *'And he shall take the hair of the head of his separation, and put it in the fire which is under the sacrifice of the peace offerings.'* The only other thing ever offered on the altar besides the burnt sacrifice was the hair of the Nazarite's separation.

Separation and the Cross

Separation flows from the Cross, and separation brings you to the Cross. If I am going to be a separated man of God I have got to come to the Cross, and if I am going to be a separated man of God I have to take up my Cross and follow Christ.

'This is the way the Master trod,
Should not His servants tread it still?'

It is the way of the Cross which leads Home. There is a separation from the world, and that separation is important today, for it seems to me that the world is infiltrating the lives, the homes and the society of those who profess the Name of Christ. Believers will do things today which twenty years ago, yes, even ten years ago, were generally condemned by the Christian Church. Why is that? Because the walls of separation are tumbling down. God help us to be totally and absolutely separated from the world. May we see to it that there is a battlement around our homes.

In the Old Testament no home was to be built without a battlement. May God help us to put up the battlement of the family altar, the exhortation of God's Word and the prayers of parents, as a battlement around our homes to keep out the world. We must see to it that the world does not reign, does not dominate, does not control, does not infiltrate our lives. We need separation in all walks of life.

Now, separation is not isolation. That is exactly what the Church of Rome does. They confound separation with isolation, so they build their monasteries and their nunneries. They build great walls to keep out the world. You will not keep out the world by building walls.

Jesus Christ was separate from sinners, yet He was the Friend of sinners. He went amongst them but His garments were unspotted by the taint of their sin. Thank God, I can walk in this world and not be of this world. I can be separated in the midst of all my mingling with men. I can be separated as a man of God walking amongst the sinful sons of men.

Ecclesiastical Separation

Then of course, there is another matter. Some people say, 'Yes, I believe in separation from the world.' There is, however, separation from ecclesiastical compromise and apostasy. Oh, when you touch this subject some people become very angry. They say, 'Oh no, we will still go to the old Church. After all, our minister is a saved man.' He may be saved, but in what Presbytery does he sit? With a group of apostates? In what union does he hold his fellowship? With men who deny the Virgin Birth and Blood of the Lamb? How can he go with God's blessing and lay hands on a man at ordination who does not believe the Word of God and who denies the fundamentals of the faith? It cannot be done in obedience to God. It is disobedience, and disobedience is sin. We can see more and more today those, who in the name of evangelism are prepared to blur the great difference between those who are saved and separated and those who are tangled up in an unholy amalgam. I cannot build the church of Antichrist, and will not. Those who say they would hold an evangelistic campaign for the Pope, if he invited them, are flying in the face of God's Holy Word. You cannot go under the sponsorship of the Devil to do the work of Jesus Christ. Let us get it straight. More and more the pressures are going to be upon us all, 'Can you not compromise just a little?'

Someone said to me, 'Now if you would just lower your flag. It is too high. Just bring it down a little and you will have more friends. People will love you more.' The only love I want is the love of God's sweet approval, and if I have got that why should I care what men think about me? Brethren and sisters in Christ, there is no such thing as degrees in separation. There is only one separation and that is the separation of this Book. What does it say? *'Touch not the unclean thing.'* Some people are kissing the unclean thing and embracing it. God says you are not to touch it even with the tip of your finger. This is the stand God has called us all to take and to maintain. We can make a stand, but it is far harder to maintain that stand down through the years. May God keep us faithful!

The Saviour's Ministry

I was greatly encouraged in reading again the life of the blessed Saviour. There is no greater example of a God anointed ministry than the ministry of the blessed Son of God. The first public act which He did after His baptism and His temptation by the Devil was the purging of the Temple. He violently cast out those who had made it a den of thieves. He did a reforming work. In the last days of His ministry He went back and did the very same thing.

There are two cleansings of the Temple, one at the beginning of His ministry and one at the end of His ministry. I have to commence my ministry by cleansing God's Temple. I have to continue my ministry by cleansing God's Temple, and I have to finish my ministry by cleansing God's Temple. There is no discharge in this war. The apostasy will ever be with us, and God's plan for clean-cut separation is ever in the Book. at the end of the day the locks of separation were to be a holy and acceptable sacrifice unto the Lord.

Could I draw a parallel? When I come to the end of the journey and stand in Heaven's Court, will I have a life of separation to offer to God as an acceptable sacrifice, gold, silver, precious stones? Or will it be wood, hay and stubble, fit only for the fire? That is the question which every one of us must ask ourselves. I for one cannot go to a Church in the World Council of Churches and have an evangelistic campaign. I cannot associate in fellowship with those who are in the great apostasy. I cannot be found on a mixed platform where you have evangelicals, pseudo-evangelicals and new-evangelicals. I cannot be there. I must be alone walking with God in the light of His Word. Of course I will be most unpopular. Of course I will be misunderstood. Of course men will say, 'He is a bigot, an extremist, a fanatic', but I must obey God rather than men.

Samson was only mighty to deliver Israel when the seven locks of separation were growing on his head.

We must keep to the Book. In running a race, any competitor can get to the winning post quickly if he breaks the rules, but the only man who gets the reward is the man who keeps to the rule book. Let us keep to the Rule Book. There are no shortcuts to God's blessing. We have got to walk the way of God. May God help us to be totally and absolutely separate from apostasy.

If you are in a Church which is in, or is in any way associated with, the World Council of Churches, stand up, shout out, get out and stay out, in the Lord's Name. That is what the Lord commands in His Book, and if you do it God will bless you.

10

THE MOTIVATION OF SAMSON

We come now to the lesson of Samson's motivation. *'And the woman bare a son, and called his name Samson; and the child grew and the Lord blessed him. And the Spirit of the Lord began to move him at times in the camp of Dan between Zorah and Eshtaol..'* Judges 13:24,25.

Some people have said they do not understand why Samson, with all his backsliding, with all his terrible sinning, with all his rebellion against the Lord, with a life punctuated with awful departures from God's commandments, should be listed among the heroes and champions of faith. If you turn to the great gallery of the champions of the faith, you will find that Samson's name is given a special place there. *'And what shall I more say, for the time would fail me to tell of Gideon, and of Barak, and of Samson; of Jephthae, of David also, and Samuel, and of the prophets.'* Hebrews 11:32.

It is easy to understand why Samson is mentioned in this galaxy of the heroes of faith. Although he had many black sins in his life, although his backslidings were tragic and terrible, and wrought awful havoc, yet Samson finished where he first began. When a man finishes where he first begins, then that man is entitled to a place among the heroes of God's work.

Judges 16:31, *'Then his brethren and all the house of his father came down, and took him, and brought him up and buried him between Zorah and Eshtaol.'* That was the very place where the Spirit of God first moved upon him. (Chapter 13:24,25). It is imperative for God's people to keep their anchorage. There must be no departure from the place where they started with God. When Abraham went down into Egypt there was no restoration for him until he came back to the place where he built the altar at the beginning.

We start at the Cross, and we must finish at the Cross. The man who does not finish where he began will not be mentioned among God's heroes of the faith. Samson, with all his backslidings and sinnings - and we dare not and must not minimise their guilt, the heinousness, the hellishness of his sinnings, finished where he began, at the place where the Spirit of God first came upon him.

The Growth of Samson

Spiritual growth is the character of a spiritual man. The apostle Paul wrote to some of his converts and said that they had need of milk and not of meat. They were not growing. They were still at the baby stage, they had never walked. They had to be carried and they had not come to the diet of manhood. We would need to ask ourselves if we, as believers, are still in babyhood.

Children are very easily offended. Did you ever see two children and each of them has a special toy, and soon one of them wants the other's toy? We had this experience in our home for we had twins, and one of them would say, 'That's my toy,' and the other would say, ' But I want it,' and then there was a free-for-all! As a minister for many years, I have seen childishness among God's people. I have seen babyhood among the saints.

Listen! Your gift will make room for itself. You do not need to push open doors. God will open the doors which need to be opened for you in Christian service. Quit your childishness! Grow up! Exchange childishness for childlikeness.

The Blessing of God

Samson grew, and *'the Lord blessed him'*. In our Authorised Version of the Bible the word LORD is spelt in small capitals, which means that in the original Hebrew text it is Jehovah, the I Am, the One who never changes, and never can change, and bless His Holy Name, never will change. *'The Lord blessed him.'*

The greatest thing any person can have is the blessing of God. That is all you need. Of course, when the Lord blesses you there will be opposition. If the Lord blesses you, the Devil's crowd will oppose you. There is nothing the Devil hates more than a man or a woman, a church or a people whom God has blessed. The Devil will oppose that person, that church, that people, and all the agents of the Devil will oppose them too.

Turn with me to that wonderful portion at the end of Genesis. Jacob is on his deathbed and calls his sons around his bed to bless them. When he comes to Joseph he records that he was hated by his brethren. There will be opposition, even in the household of faith, to the man that God blesses. *'Joseph is a fruitful bough.'* When God blesses you, you will be fruitful. There will be results to your ministry. The greatest testimony that a minister of Christ can have is the fruit which results from his ministry. The fruit does not come because of anything he does. It comes because of God's sovereign blessing. If God wants to pick up a man, or a church, or a people, and bless them, nothing can stop the blessing of God. God is sovereign in His blessing of His people. *'Joseph is a fruitful bough by a well.'* He is by a well of living water. This bough did not bear fruit of itself. The richness and the refreshment which it needed came from the well. What does it say about Joseph? *'whose branches run over the wall,'* so when God blesses a man nobody can limit or circumscribe his ministry. No one can circumscribe the ministry of a man whom God blesses; his branches will run over the wall.

Vain attempts to circumscribe a God-blessed ministry

When the Lord started to bless me in my ministry, after a day and a night of prayer in the old Church, there were people who wanted to circumscribe my ministry. They told me I was not to go and take evangelistic services. Certain members of my Church Committee said to me, 'If you go and take evangelistic services we will not pay you and we will not pay the men who come to preach for you. You will have to pay your own supplies.' I said, 'Well, if that's all you are worrying about I will do that.' Yes, and I did it for years. I paid the pulpit supply of every man who came to preach when I was away evangelising. We had a treasurer and when I went away for a gospel campaign he even stopped paying the Church's share of my national insurance! Then one day there was an election and all those skinflints were thrown off the Committee and men who were generous took their place. These men believed that their minister's branches should run over the wall. No one can stop a person whom the Lord blesses. His branches run over the wall. What happens? Who opposes him? His brethren! Who opposed Joseph? The Devil's agent, Potiphar, and his wife, but who were the most bitter in their opposition? His own brethren!

This preacher has been sorely shot at, and has been grieved, not by the darts that came from the Devil's armoury, but by the darts which came from the quivers carried by his own brethren, especially brethren whom this preacher helped and supported and strengthened. The Lord said, 'Your bow will abide in strength, and I will continue to bless you,' That is all I care about, to know God's blessing.

If I have God's blessing in my ministry nobody can stop me, but when I cease to have God's blessing then I am absolutely finished. So it does not matter which one of the household of faith takes the bitter arrow and fires it to grieve this preacher, if God blesses me I will be blessed and my branches will run over the wall.

To the ends of the earth the ministry of this Church has gone. Why? Because the Lord said, 'I am going to bless that preacher.' It is not because there was anything in me. God can remove the candlestick at any time. '*The wind bloweth where it listeth*,' and it is God's purpose to bless. I will tell you something more, the gifts and calling of God are without repentance. When God deigns to bless His child, he will be blessed indeed.

Look at verse 25. Notice the blessings which he will have, '*The blessings of heaven above; blessings of the deep that lieth under; blessings of the breasts, and of the womb; and the blessings of thy father.'* Genesis 49:25,26. There are five blessing, because five is the number of grace. The Holy Spirit always has His numbers right. There will be the blessings of heaven, the blessings of the deep, the blessings of the breasts, the blessings of the womb, and the blessings of thy father. Look at what it says about Joseph, *'They shall be on the head of Joseph, and on the crown of the head of him that was separate from his brethren.'* God's separated man will have God's blessing. That is what happened to Samson.

The Spirit of God

You will find another most interesting thing about Samson. Something happened to him. This is the point which we must emphasise, *'the Spirit of the Lord began to move him at times in the camp of Dan.'* He was not always moved by the Spirit of God. God's servant does not always move with a mighty breath of Heaven. The Spirit Himself is also sovereign. Oh, for the blessed times when the Spirit of God begins to move upon His people, between Zorah and Eshtaol.

Eshtaol means a valley, a low place; and Zorah means a prominent place. This is of course a perfect type of the pilgrimage of the child of God. At times we are down in the valley, at other times we are on the mountain top.

The Spirit of God can move upon you when you are down in the valley. Sometimes we are on the mountain top and the sun is shining and everything is going well, and the Spirit of God can move upon us on the mountain top. There is also an in-between place, a place between the valley and the heights. It is in the in-between place that we most need God to keep us by the strength of His arm.

We should note carefully how many times the Spirit of God came upon Samson. At the end of the day he had a final anointing of the Spirit of God and slew more in his death than in his life.

What is our motivation? Is it selfish? Is it to be heard, is it to be seen, is to have notoriety just for the sake of it, or is our motivation guided by the Lord? Is it the Spirit who is pushing us forward to do the will and work of God?

May God help us to realise three things: (i) we need spiritual growth; (ii) we need spiritual blessing; and above all (iii) we need the Holy Spirit Himself. That was the secret of Samson's strength, and this will be the secret of our strength if we are going to defeat the uncircumcised Philistines of our day.

11

THE ASSOCIATION OF SAMSON

The lesson of Samson's association is found in chapter 14. There is an old saying that a man is known by the company he keeps, and alas, in the sad story of Samson's tragedy we see that his association led to his temptation and eventually to his degradation and shame.

Going down

In chapter 14:1 there is a very suggestive phrase, *'Samson went down.'* Underline that phrase. Verse five, *'Then went Samson down.'* Verse 7, *'and he went down.'* That very suggestive phrase occurs three times. Three in scripture is the number of completion, so we have the complete downgrade of Samson suggested in the repetition of that phrase.

Next, look at the place to which he went down. *'He went down to Timnath.'*

Timnath means 'the place of the vineyard.' Samson was a Nazarite. He was not to associate himself in any way with the fruit of the vine or the juice of the grape. Here Samson is going down into the very place of temptation, to the very trees that were forbidden him, to the very place where there grew the fruit of the vine and where that fruit was pressed for the making of wine. He went and associated himself with a place of dangerous exposure to sin.

If we are going to maintain our separation unto the Lord, if we are going to live in a God honouring way, if we are going to tread the highway of holiness and the path of truth, then we must not go down and make associations in dangerous places with the world, the flesh and the Devil. If we do so, such associations will lead to temptations, and those temptations will lead to our ruination before God. We have to flee from all appearance of evil. I know no chapters in the Bible so sad as the chapters which record the descent of God's people into backsliding.

You will find in the Book of Genesis the fact that Abraham went down into Egypt. It was a going down. It was retrogression and not progression. Egypt in the Bible is a type of the world, and the world is no friend to grace, and will not help us on to God.

The Flesh Prevailed

Secondly, in his association the flesh prevailed. Samson decided on a mixed marriage. He thought to take as his wife a woman of the Philistines. No good ever comes of mixed marriages. Could I relate to every young person something I heard Archdeacon T C Hammond, the great Protestant protagonist, the greatest our islands have ever seen in this generation, 'Marry your own! Marry your own!' We would need to re-echo that to the ends of the Kingdom today. No good comes of mixed marriages. Could I carry it one degree further? If you are a believer and you know Christ as your Saviour, then you should only marry in the Lord. Any other marriage is a mixed marriage and an unequal yoke, and God cannot bless it or honour it. We should all be guided by the clear instructions of the Bible.

There was one thing which prevailed upon Samson. It was not the good pleasure of God or the approbation of the Almighty. He kept saying, *'She pleaseth me well.'* Judges 14:3). He put his pleasure and gratification before the command of God Almighty. If we elevate the flesh, if we allow the flesh to dictate our pathway, if we allow the flesh to govern our minds, our hearts, our wills and our conduct, then we are heading for ruin and disaster. We must learn well the lesson of Samson and his association. He went down. He went into the place where he was exposed to danger in the vineyard. He adopted plans for a mixed marriage. He allowed the flesh to prevail. His motivation was not the Spirit of God but the fact that this woman pleased him well.

The Prefiguration of Samson

Let us turn now to another lesson, the lesson of Samson's prefiguration. This is one of the most interesting parts in any study of the life of Samson.

First, a word of instruction in regard to the study of Old Testament types, shadows and symbols. Many of the Old Testament characters are types of the Lord Jesus Christ, but there is one thing you need to keep clearly before you in any study of the Old Testament characters as a type of Christ -

they are never types of Christ as far as their characters are concerned. Christ is the holy, sinless, spotless, crimeless, fault-less Son of God. Everyone else is stained, soiled, scarred and marred with sin, so never in their character are they types of the Lord Jesus Christ. If you keep that before you it will keep you steady as a rock in your interpretation of Old testament characters as types of Christ.

How are they types of Christ? They are types of Christ only in their circumstances. We find in four circumstances that Samson is a beautiful type of Christ.

First Prefiguration

When Samson was in Timnath in the vineyards, *'behold, a young lion roared against him. And the Spirit of the Lord came mightily upon him, and he rent him as he would have rent a kid, and he had nothing in his hand.'* Chapter 14:15. This incident in the life of Samson is at the beginning of his career. In the parallel to the life of Christ what was the first thing in Christ's career after His baptism? It was His temptation in the wilderness. The lion of hell roared against the blessed Son of God. Samson had nothing in his hand. The Lord Jesus Christ had nothing in His hand when He met the Devil in that great temptation in the wilderness. What weapon did He use? The Word of God.

Where the first Adam fell the last Adam triumphed, and where the first Adam turned a paradise into a wilderness, the last Adam turned a wilderness into a paradise. So we have here in Samson a foreshadowing, a prefiguration of Christ.

Second Prefiguration

The second prefiguration you will find in chapter 15:9-

20. Samson is to be betrayed. Who betrays him? The men of Judah (v.11). Who betrayed the Lord Jesus Christ? Judas (or Judah). Notice carefully the parallel. *'the men of Judah came to betray Samson.'* Judas Iscariot betrayed the Lord. What happened? When Samson was delivered into the hands of the Philistines he reached for the jawbone of an ass, and with that jawbone he slew heaps upon heaps of Philistines, and there was a great slaughter and a great deliverance.

Tell me, what is the power which Jesus Christ uses to slay his enemies? It is the jawbone of an ass. It is the preaching of the Word of God which slays the enemies of the gospel. To those ot the world the preacher is only an ass, he is only a donkey. They think he is a fool. It has pleased God through the foolishness of preaching to save them that believe. God has ordained that by the preaching of His Word heaps upon heaps of the enemies of God will be subdued by the power of the gospel. Notice something else - after Samson had slain the Philistines God clave a hollow place that was in the jaw, *'And there came water thereout; and when he had drunk, his spirit came again, and he was revived.'* (v.19). What is it which revives the preacher after the battle? Nothing other than the precious water from the very Word which he has himself been preaching. That is the refreshing draught which slakes his thirst, a wonderful prefiguration of the work of Jesus Christ.

Third Prefiguration

The third prefiguration you will find in chapter 16. The men of Gaza have barred the gate, they have closed the door. Midnight has come, and they think they have Samson imprisoned for ever.

Gaza is a type of the tomb. The Lord Jesus Christ lay in the tomb and the door was shut. The great stone rolled to the sepulchre was sealed with all the military strength which Rome and the Pharisees could muster. It seemed that Samson was going to perish, and it seemed that the body of Christ would be held in prison for ever. The mighty Samson rose at midnight and laid the doors of the gates, and the bar and the posts upon his shoulders, and carried them up to the top of the hill of Hebron. The Mightier than Samson went to the door of the tomb and burst forever the doors of death. He laid the bar and the posts of death upon His shoulders and carried them up to the Hill of God, and at the girdle of Christ today there hang the keys of hell and of death. Jesus is Victor over the tomb. Its doors are burst forever for the people of God. That is why we can sing -

Death cannot keep his prey,
Jesus my Saviour!
He tore the bars away,
Jesus my Lord!
Up from the grave He arose,
With a mighty triumph o'er His foes;
He arose a Victor from the dark domain,
And He lives forever with His saints to reign.
He arose! He arose! Hallelujah! Christ arose!

Hallelujah! Christ is alive for evermore!
Up in heaven today at the chariot wheels of the Mighty Christ there lies the monument of death, smashed and broken and conquered for His people for evermore.
When did He rise? He arose after midnight, early on the first day of the week.

The Fourth Prefiguration

The fourth prefiguration is recorded in the last great act in the drama of Samson's life. Chapter 16:26-30 tells of the death of Samson. Where did he die? He died amongst his enemies. Where did the Lord Jesus Christ die? He died amongst His enemies. Samson had only one friend in that great crowd, and that was the little lad who led him. Christ had only one friend at the Cross, and that was the dying thief who said, *'Lord remember me when Thou comest into Thy Kingdom.'*

Jesus Christ made His grave with the wicked. So did Samson make his grave with the wicked. In his death Samson pulled down the temple of false religion and laid in ruin for ever the temples of the adversary. So by His death, Jesus Christ pulled down for ever the temples of paganism, antichrist and false religions, and as He died He cried *'It is finished!'* and the work was done and done for evermore. From among the ruins the tender hands of Samson's friends took his body for burial. From the ruin of the Cross Nicodemus and Joseph of Arimathea took the precious body of the Lord.

They laid Samson in a special tomb, the tomb of his fathers. They laid my Lord in a tomb where never man was laid. Christ had a virgin birth and Christ had a virgin burial. He lay in a tomb where never man had lain. Of Samson it is said *'He slew more in his death than in his life.'* Of my blessed Saviour it can be said *'By His death, life and immortality have been brought to light through the gospel.'*

May the Lord teach us the wonderful lessons of the prefigurations of Christ in the life of Samson.

If you as yet have not learned the secret of Divine redemption and forgiveness, you can pass from death to life and from the power of sin and Satan unto God by coming to Christ and trusting in His blood.

12

THE CONFRONTATION
OF SAMSON

We now turn to the lesson of Samson's confrontation. Chapter 15:4,5, *'And Samson went, and caught three hundred foxes, and took firebrands, and turned tail to tail, and put a firebrand in the midst between two tails. and when he had set the brands on fire, he let them go into the standing corn of the Philistines, and burnt up both the shocks, and also the standing corn, with the vineyards and olives.'*

Notice that in his confrontation with the enemy, Samson attacked their fruits, their harvests, their vineyards and their fields.

In the great battle which is raging today between Christ and Antichrist, in the great battle between the forces of evangelicalism and the forces of ecumenism, it is the duty, the bounden duty of God's believing people to attack the harvest fields and the fruits of the great apostasy. The harvest field has got to be invaded by the swordsmen of the Lord. Those places which are bringing forth a ripening harvest of the seed of apostasy have got to be destroyed by the power of the gospel. There is need for militancy. There is need for aggression. There is need for the Church to take the offensive against the enemy. How many Churches are content with a rearguard action! How many Churches are content just to defend their own boundary, to hold to their own, to keep their own little territory quiet and peaceful!

The lesson we learn from this Book is the complete destruction of the fruits and harvest of the enemies of the gospel. 2 Corinthians 10:4,5, *'The weapons of our warfare are not carnal, but mighty through God to the pulling down of the strongholds.'* When I talk about attacking the fruits of apostasy I am not talking about a physical resistance of those fruits. I am talking about a spiritual resistance of those fruits. I am not talking about physical confrontation. I am talking about spiritual confrontation. *'For the weapons of our warfare are not carnal, but mighty through God to the pulling down of strong holds; casting down imaginations, and every high thing that exalteth itself against the knowledge of God, and bringing into captivity every thought to the obedience of Christ."*

The Lord uses the most unusual methods to accomplish His work, and in this Book of Judges we have some of these methods recorded. I must confess I like this man Samson. I wish he were around today. I would like to be his servant while he dealt with the enemies of the gospel.

Total war against the fruits of apostasy

First of all, Samson set about the job of catching three hundred foxes. (Three hundred is a very important number in the Book of Judges. When Gideon was going to deliver the children of Israel he had only three hundred men who lapped. Three in scripture is the number of completion).

That was some task to begin with, and then he took them two by two, tied their tails together and put a firebrand between their tails. So now he had one hundred and fifty pairs of foxes with lighted brands tied to their tails. There must have been some screams and howls from those foxes when Samson lit the brands! I'm sure those foxes were raring to go! He let them off and directed them into the standing corn of the Philistines. What was he doing? He was carrying the fire into the harvest field of the enemy.

Of course, if the World Council of Churches had been around they would have passed a resolution against this bigoted man Samson who had no evangelical love. They would have said that he couldn't have been God's man to do such a thing. But Samson had everything to do with God. Jenny Geddis, who had a four-legged stool which she threw at the massing priest in St. Giles' Cathedral in Edinburgh, was God's woman.

It is about time God's people got away from false respectability and were prepared to use the weapons which God puts into their hands.

What a hubbub there would have been among the so-called evangelicals of our day if they had been around in Samson's day! Can't you see the corn beginning to burn and the Philistines calling out the fire engines, but all to no avail. The harvest lay in ruins; their vineyards were burnt; their olive trees were burnt. It was a total, utter and complete destruction. *'Destroy them utterly'* says the Book, and Samson did just that.

Learn this lesson today. It is the duty of the true man of God to declare war upon the fruits of the harvest of apostasy.

Total war against the apostates themselves

Turn to chapter 15:14-17. There Samson not only attacked the fruits of the apostasy but he attacked the apostates themselves. Now we are told that we should not mention anybody when we are denouncing doctrinal errors. It is all very well to deal with the unbelief of modernism but do not name a modernist! It is all very well to deal with the deception of ecumenism, but do not name an ecumenist! It is all very well to deal with the superstition and priestcraft of Popery, but do not name the protagonists of this antichrist system! The philosophy of naming the enemy, we are told, is completely contrary to God's Word.

There was a young preacher called Timothy, and there was an old teacher called Paul. Paul was writing to Timothy and warning him about apostates. Did he name them? Did he deal generally with their doctrinal apostasy or did he name them? Turn to 1 Timothy 1:18, *'This charge I commit unto thee, son Timothy, according to the prophecies which went before on thee, that thou by them mightest war a good warfare.'* How do you war a good warfare? *'Holding faith, and a good conscience; which some having put away concerning faith have made shipwreck: of whom is Hymenaeus and Alexander.'* Paul named them. He did not deal in generalities. He individualised, and that is what we have got to do. We have got to individualise and deal with the apostasy. *'Of whom is Hymenaeus and Alexander, whom I have delivered unto Satan, that they may learn not to blaspheme.'* Paul openly named these two men in a public service and handed them over in the Name of the Father, Son, and Holy Spirit, to the Devil. That is the way we need to deal with apostates.

In the first chapter of 2 Timothy you will also find that when Paul mentions the great apostasy he names two more men, v.15, '*This thou knowest, that all they which are in Asia be turned away from me; of whom are Phygellus and Hermogenes.*' He is naming names again!

In chapter 2:17 he names two others, Hymenaeus and Philetus. In chapter 3 he tells us the names, which have not been given before, of the man and his wife who opposed Moses down in Egypt. (Jannes is the man's name and Jambres is the woman's name). '*Now as Jannes and Jambres withstood Moses, so do these also resist the truth.*'

In 2 Tim. 4:14 he names another man, '*Alexander the coppersmith did me much evil: the Lord reward him according to his works.*'

The apostates have got to be named. That is what this Book says. It does not matter what I think or what I would like to do, or what is not pleasing to the flesh, but rather what is obedience to God.

Total war against the defences of apostasy

Chapter 16:1-3 we find that Samson attacks their defences. He first attacks their fruits, then their persons, and then their defences. He is down in Gaza, and we read, '*And he lay till midnight, and arose at midnight, and took the doors of the gate of the city, and the two posts, and went away with them.*'

It is our duty to attack the defences, the gates and the posts of the great apostasy, to make a 'breaking and entering' into their defences, to carry the battle not only to the gates but through the gates into the citadels of apostasy. God has called us to fight the good fight of faith, and to war a good warfare. We are in a battle. There is nothing pleasant about it, nothing easy about it, nothing pleasing to the flesh about it, but it is the way in which God would have us go.

Alas, today there are so few prepared to bear the reproach and do the job thoroughly. In the days of Cromwell there was a branch of the Puritans which was known as the 'root and branch' men. They believed in rooting out popery, root and branch. We need a lot of root and branch men in the church today to attack the citadels of apostasy and to battle against the hordes of hell, to carry the ramparts of their citadels, to break in their doors so that men and women held captive by the devil at his will, can be released and know the emancipation and freedom of the gospel.

Total war against the religion of apostasy

Finally, you will notice that Samson's last act was to attack their religion, chapter 16:28-30.

The last attack he made was in the citadel, the shrine, the temple of Dagon.

I have to attack the fruits of apostasy. I have to attack the persons of the apostates. I have to attack the defences of apostasy and I have to attack the shrine, the inner circle, the very place where the apostate holds his worship. I have got to carry the battle right into the ranks of the enemy.

I see the mighty Samson with strength renewed, the Spirit of God coming upon him again, and he pushes apart the great pillars of the temple, and Dagon's temple tumbles to the ground, and great is the fall thereof.

There is no discharge in this war. There is no easy way for any one of us. I must finish the battle the way I commenced it, with the sword out of its scabbard, dripping with the blood of the enemies of those who resist Jesus Christ. Brethren and sisters, the battle is going to become more difficult in the coming days. The battle for truth is going to become more demanding. There is going to be more hatred and more reproach and more bitterness against those who stand for God and truth. Compromise is the order of the day amongst evangelicals and pseudo-fundamentalists.

Some years ago I was preaching in Philadelphia, and the IRA had a picket line outside the church. They carried posters saying 'Paisley is a murderer'. The man who organised that picket was just forty-four years of age. A few days after I came home I received a message from the minister of the Church to say that that man had fallen dead.

I am a nothing and a nobody, but do not put your hand against God's work. Do not stand against those who stand for God, because the Lord will fight for those who stand for Him and woe be to all their opponents.

May God make us strong in these evil days for His Name's sake.

13

THE TEMPTATION, DEGRADATION AND RESTORATION OF SAMSON

We want to look at three other lessons in the life of Samson, the lesson of his temptation, the lesson of his degradation and the lesson of his restoration. Chapter 16 is a sad chapter. It is a dark chapter. It is a chapter in which God puts up the beacon light of warning to every one of us, warning us of the pitfalls, warning us of the nets, warning us of the reefs that lie ahead for any believer who deviates from God's revealed will. There is always danger, there is always darkness, and there is always disaster when a man of God or a woman of God goes outside God's revealed will.

Samson's Temptation

Notice in verse 4 that once again Samson's besetting sin, the sin over which he was never able to triumph, the sin of

the flesh, rises once again. He is on dangerous ground.
Look at the valley of Sorek. The word Sorek means 'the place
of the vine with dusky-coloured grapes'. Samson was a
Nazarite. He ought not to have gone where the grapes were
growing, for if the fruit of the grape had passed his lips he
would have been robbed of the great strength which the Spirit
of God had imparted to him. Samson got onto dangerous
ground.

Dear believer, we should shun the dangerous ground.
When God has put up warning signs in His Word we should
take heed. So often today Christians take a chance. They say
'We will not be straight-laced. We will not be Puritanical. We
will be open-minded. We will take a risk.' In God's name
heed the warning signs of the Book, and shun all appearance
of evil.

We read that Samson got in touch with the harlot Delilah.
The name Delilah means 'languishing'. Of course, once we
cultivate an association which is outside God's will our
spiritual life begins to languish. Why is it that the prayer life
of God's people is languishing today? Because there is an
association in their life which is God dishonouring, which is
flying in the very face of God's revealed will. Why is it that
the power in the Church is languishing? Because the members of the Church are in an unholy fellowship with those
things that God Almighty has forbidden.

We would need to major on a series of messages on the
sins of the saints, because today we have the saints of God
besmirched with the sins of the world, the sins of the flesh
and the sins of the Devil. We need to guard ourselves against
such things, perfecting holiness in the fear of God. Languishing spiritual life is the result when the Church flirts with the
Delilahs of this age.

Andrew Bonar said, 'I look for the Church and I find it in the world. I look for the world, and I find it in the Church.'

There are three things about the temptation which Samson faced:

(i) Delusive Temptation

First of all, it was a delusive temptation. It promised pleasure. It promised excitement. It promised satisfaction, but instead it brought death.

Look at verse 16, *'His soul was vexed unto death.'* If you glance in the margin it reads, *'his soul was shortened unto death.'* The temptations of the world, the flesh and the Devil are delusive. The Devil promises you pleasure, satisfaction, enjoyment, excitement, but there is no lasting satisfaction with the Devil's pleasure and sin. The world's excitements are short-lived. The world's joys come speedily to an end. A delusive temptation! Samson learned that! He learned it in the bitterness of dark experience.

(ii) Deceptive Temptation

Secondly, the temptation was deceptive, deceiving Samson that he could go into Delilah's house and still come out with God's power. There are preachers today who think they can remain in the great apostasy; they think they can remain in the World Council of Churches; they think they can remain in Delilah's house, the harlot temple of apostasy, and retain their power. It is a deception of the Devil. There is only one place of power and that is outside the camp, where Jesus is.

I get really sick of people who tell me that God has told them to disobey the direct commands of scripture. God never told anyone to do that. it was the Devil who told them to do it. When God says 'Come out' He does not mean 'Stay in'. When God says 'Avoid' He does not mean 'Associate with'. When God says 'Touch not' He does not mean 'Embrace'.

Any man who comes along, no matter how nice he may be, and tells me that God has instructed him to disobey God's Holy Word, is deceived. Here we have Samson deceived. He thought he could retain his power and yet sin. You cannot do it. You sin and you will lose your power. You flirt with the Devil's crowd and you will lose your power. You associate with evil and evil will rob you of your strength.

(iii) Diabolical Temptation

Thirdly, this temptation was diabolical. It started to intrude into the very secret of Samson's power. First of all, the green withs were taken to bind him, then the new ropes were taken to bind him. Eventually the power of the Devil crept into the very place where his power was, into the seven locks of his hair. He said to Delilah, *'Weave them into your web'* , and what happened? He was getting nearer to revealing his secret.

The Devil's power starts subtilly. It moves silently, and at the end it moves stealthily on to satanic triumph.

I know no more dark picture in all the Bible than this 16th chapter of the Book of Judges.

Samson's Degradation

I want you to notice the lesson of his degradation. Samson eventually revealed all that was in his heart. Delilah said to the Philistines 'Come up', and they brought the money in their hands. She put Samson to sleep and then called a man, and off came the characteristics of Samson's separation, his seven locks of hair. When the Christian loses his separation he has lost the enduement of the Spirit of God. He has lost his power. He has lost his testimony.

However, there is one thing which a Christian cannot lose, he cannot lose his soul. Thank God for that! If it was left to our own agency we would lose our soul, but thank God our soul is in the keeping of the One who shall keep it spotless until the day of His appearing.

A Christian can lose everything but his soul, and that is what Samson did. What degradation is here! I think the saddest verse in this whole Book is verse 20, when Samson said, *'I will go out as at other times before, and shake myself.'* He went through the old system, he did the old performance, but *'he wist not that the Spirit of the Lord was departed from him'.* He wist not that he was a God-forsaken man.

Many a preacher goes through the old performance, through the old way of doing things, but he does not know that the Spirit of God has gone. There is a day when the Spirit of God says 'Good-bye' to a disobedient believer, when He no longer imparts His power because of the sin which that believer is committing. That is what Paul meant when he said, *'lest I become a castaway.'* - a reject, someone put on the shelf, a useless, an obsolete article for which God Almighty has no more time.

Brethren and sisters, this is what the devil aims at, to put us all on the shelf so that we will be useless in the future to do God's work in God's way.

Samson did not know that the Lord had departed. What happened to him? First, he lost his vision. Secondly, he lost his liberty, and lastly, he became a bondslave of the Devil, doing the devil's work. That is what happens to a person who goes out of God's revealed will, they lose their vision, their liberty and their Master.

Vision Gone

I see the branding iron heated white hot in the fire. I see those Philistines laying Samson on the ground, holding him down, and I see the tip of that branding iron touching each of his eyes. There is a terrible scream from his anguished, agonised soul, and his vision is gone!

Sin puts out the eyes of God's people. That is why they no longer see the souls who are going to hell. That is why they no longer have any urge to attend the prayer meetings. 'Where there is no vision the people perish.' Has the Devil put out your eyes?

If God's people saw the need of sinners today would they not be urgent to bring them under the sound of the gospel that they might hear the living, saving Word of God ? Alas, many come to God's house on their own and never say to a neighbour, a friend or a loved one, 'You are a perishing soul. Come with me and hear words whereby you can be saved.' Vision is gone! I think this Church is in danger of losing its vision. When I see the vast number of my members who will not give fifteen minutes of their time on a Sabbath evening to help souls to Christ, it breaks my heart as a preacher, and if it breaks this human heart of mine, how much it must break the heart of the Lord Christ who bled on Calvary to bring men to Christ. We have a job to do. Let us do it. May God restore to us the vision!

Liberty gone

Secondly, Samson lost his liberty. Brass in scripture is the symbol of judgment. They bound him with fetters of brass. It is a terrible thing for the child of God to be under the judgment of the world. Here the world, the enemies of Jehovah, bound the mighty Samson, the man who once had such power that they could not do anything to hold him. Now he is held in fetters of brass.

Nothing will rob you of your liberty like breaking God's commandments. Sin is bondage, and *'sin when it is finished, bringeth forth death.'*

Why are God's people not enjoying the liberty of Christ, the joy of the Lord and the fire of gospel truth? Because the devil has taken from them their liberty.

Serving the Devil

Thirdly, not only was there spiritual blindness and spiritual bondage for Samson, but also spiritual barrenness. What does he do? He grinds in the prison house. That is a good word, 'grind'. There are lots of Christians and as far as God's service is concerned they are just grinding. It is a dreadful bore for them! What an effort they need to make to come to one service on the Lord's Day. Suggest to them that they should go to a prayer meeting and they say they are too busy. God's children have room for pleasure, room for business, but they have no room for God. Perhaps, child of God, you had better understand that the Lord has departed from you. You had better find out what is wrong with you. The greatest tragedy of all is a backslidden Christian who doesn't know he is backslidden, and away from God. He does not realize that he is without God's power!

Service! How grinding can God's service be when you are outside the will of God! No motivation, no joy, you do not waken on the Lord's Day morning and say, 'Praise God, it is the Lord's Sabbath. I am going to have a day in God's Courts.' You do not waken on Wednesday and say,'Thank God, this is prayer meeting night. I am going along to get my battery charged. I am going along to get more joy and power and blessing from the Word.' Believer, you had better face up to your spiritual condition and position.

Samson went and shook himself as at other times, but he wist not that the Spirit of God had departed from him.

Samson's Restoration

Thank God, there is the lesson of Samson's restoration. How good, longsuffering and merciful is our God!

Separation Restored

Notice that the first thing he had to recover was his separation. Verse 22, *'Howbeit the hair of his head began to grow again after he was shaven.'*

Until you recover your separation you can never be restored to the Lord. You must start again where you left off. Abraham, when he made that disastrous descent into Egypt, had to come back and build again the altar in the same place as he had built it at the beginning. Where does a backslider start again? He starts where he left off. Separation, back to the seven locks of hair, the mark of the Nazarite, back to nailing my colours to the masthead and declaring, 'I am a child of God, a separated child of God. I must walk the way of the Lord. I cannot walk any more in the way of the world. I must walk in the way of God's commandments.'

Supplication Restored

The second thing is supplication. You will never get back to the Lord until you start praying again. Notice that Samson started to pray. What was his prayer? *'Remember me.'* That is a wonderful prayer. That is what the dying thief prayed, *'Lord remember me.'* When God's people start asking God to remember them, then they are on their way in deed and in truth.

Samson thought he could do without God, but he could not, and now he says, *'Lord remember me.'* How sweet is that prayer in the ear of Deity, when a backslider says, 'Lord remember me.'

Then he said, *'Strengthen me.'* That is exactly what he needed. He had become weak. He prayed for the very thing he needed. 'Strengthen me.' I have been robbed of my strength, O God, I have gone to sleep on the harlot's lap. I have lost my separation, my eyes, my testimony, O God strengthen me.'

He was not praying for something which did not come out of the soul agony of his broken heart. It was a heart-rending prayer. He continues, 'Strengthen me, just this once. They have put out my eyes, taken away my vision. O God avenge me. Avenge me, thy servant, because they have robbed me of a vision of Thyself.'

God is jealous for the vision of Himself. There is one thing which will waken up the strength of God on behalf of His people, and that is when the Devil and his hosts try to blot out from His people a vision of Himself. God is jealous for Himself.

Sacrifice Restored

The last thing I want you to notice is sacrifice. Samson did not ask that his life would be preserved. He said, 'I will die with the Philistines. I will pay the price.' Separation, supplication, sacrifice, that is the way back to God. Yes, there is a price to be paid. There is a Cross to be faced and carried. There must be a yielding to God's commands. What happened? Samson took his hands which had been powerless, but God had restored their power, and he put one hand against one pillar and one hand against the other pillar and bowed himself. The great crowd roared with glee saying, 'He has got no power.'   Suddenly cracks appeared on the outer skin of the pillars, and then those cracks became yawning chasms.   Terror and anguish came; screams burst forth from the mouths of the great multitude of sport-makers; the gigantic temple structure began to rock.   Soon its mass of masonry collapsed, its falling wooden beams crashed upon the heads of those who had mocked Samson and his God. Samson killed more in his death than in his life.

When God restores He really restores. He kills the fatted calf for the prodigal. He puts the best robe upon him. He gives him the best place in the house. God does all things well for the child of God who comes back to Him.

I have often wondered why the Spirit of God put Samson's name into the eleventh chapter of Hebrews. He could well have left him out, but He did not. There in the great chapter of the heroes of faith Samson's name is recorded. *'Time would fail me to tell of Samson and of Gideon.'* Why? You find the key in verse 31, because the place where he started was the place where he finished, *'Then his brethren and all the house of his father came down, and took him, and brought him up, and buried him between Zorah and Eshtaol.'*

In what place did he receive the enduement with power? Between Zorah and Eshtaol. Where did he finish? He finished in the burying place of Manoah, between Zorah and Eshtaol. He got back to where he was at the beginning. That was the proof that he was a real man of God, and that is why his name is engraved in gold in the great galaxy of the heroes and heroines of the faith in Hebrews chapter eleven.

If I am going to do anything for God I must come back to where I was at the beginning. I trust that we will come back to where we were at the beginning.

14

CORRUPT MORALS, CORRUPT RELIGION, CORRUPT PRIESTS, AND CORRUPT FAITH

We have dealt with the judges, those striking persons whom God raised up to do a special and specific work. We now come to the last five chapters of Joshua, chapters 17 -21. The key to those chapters is found in chapters 17:6; 18:1; 19:1; and 21:25.

Chapter 17:6, *'In those days there was no king in Israel, but every man did that which was right in his own eyes.'*

Chapter 18:1, *'In those days there was no king in Israel.'*

Chapter 19:1, *'And it came to pass in those days, when there was no king in Israel.'*

Chapter 21:25, *'In those days there was no king in Israel; every man did that which was right in his own eyes.'*

It was an age of lawlessness. There was no royal authority. There was no obedience or conformity to God's law. These chapters reveal the darkness, the degradation and the debauchery which resulted from rebellion against God's law. It was a state of sinful and atrocious anarchy.

In concluding this exposition I want to be both short and suggestive. These chapters highlight corruption in morals. They highlight corruption in religion. They highlight corruption in the priesthood, and they highlight corruption in faith.

Corruption of Morals

First of all, look at the corruption in morals, chapter 17:2. This man Micah was a thief. He stole from his mother. Although he kept a house of gods, although he professed adherence to religious principles, although he made a fair show in the outward religious pattern, yet he was a thief. Mark also that he only returned the money he had stolen from his mother because he was afraid of the curse. It was not out of any true repentance of heart or because of any work of grace in his heart, but rather out of a slavish fear of the curse. Notice also the strange language which his mother used. She said of him, the thief, *'Blessed be thou of the Lord, my son.'*

There is nothing blessed of God in the breaking of God's commandments. God made two tables of His law. The first table had five commandments on it, what man is to believe concerning God. The second table had five commandments on it, what duties God requires of man. One of the commandments is this, *'Thou shalt not steal.'* Here is a thief and his mother turns to him and says, 'Blessed be thou of the Lord, my son.'

We live in a day when people think they can get the blessing of God by violating God's commandments. We live in a day of corrupted morals.

There are people who say that the Lord told them to do certain things, but when we examine the Scriptures we find their plain teaching is directly opposed to what those people are doing, yet they maintain that the Lord told them to do it, and they ask God's blessing on it. You cannot have God's blessing in this way. What God says in His Book must be obeyed, and all the religious phraseology, all the nice pious talk, cannot cover the sin of your heart.

We live in a day when men fly in the face of God's Word and then they profess to know God's blessing. It cannot be. It is a counterfeit. It is a deception. To say the Lord told you to do something contrary to God's Word is making God a liar. God does not lie. What He says stands forever. Nothing can be added to it and nothing can be taken from it. Our day is like the days in the Book of Judges. There is corruption of morals.

Corruption of Religion

In verse 5 we find that Micah was corrupted religiously. This man who had Jehovah's Name on his lips and upon them so often, was corrupt religiously. He was always conversing about the Lord and yet he *'had a house of gods and made an ephod, and teraphim, and consecrated one of his sons, who became his priest.'* On the first table of the law it was written, *'Thou shalt not make unto thee any graven image.'*

Micah violated the second table of the law. He was a thief. He was also an idolator. Corrupt morals always lead to idolatry. An idolatrous man is an immoral man, for idolatry is immorality in worship, and it leads to immorality in practice. The idolatrous pagan nations of the world are immoral nations, and where Rome rules supreme with her idolatry, then immorality is rampant.

I was in Rome at the Second Vatican Council along with Revs. John Wylie and John Douglas. We were under police surveillance. At the end of the first day of the Vatican Council I said to the detectives who were with us that we would like to go and stand at the Vatican and watch the Cardinals coming out. We went to Vatican Square. After the pomp and ceremony of the opening session of the Vatican Council, we saw the Cardinals coming out. What else did we see? We saw the prostitutes lined up and the cardinals choosing which one they wanted. I asked the detective what this was all about and he said, 'It's the Cardinals going on their honeymoon,' and he laughed. We live in a day when the Church of Rome poses in this country as a strong moral influence. There is nothing moral about idolatry. It leads to the grossest of sins and to the darkest blotches of immorality.

I was speaking to a missionary from Brazil and I asked him, 'Who are the most immoral people in Brazil?' He said, 'It is easy to answer that. The priests of the Roman Catholic church are the most immoral people in Brazil.' Where there is immorality there is idolatry, and where there is idolatry there is immorality. We have it in this seventeenth chapter of Judges. Here was a man with a house of gods and yet his heart was totally and utterly corrupt.

Notice what he wanted to do. He wanted to put Jehovah among his gods. In verse 3 when he restored the eleven hundred shekels of silver to his mother, she said, '*I had wholly dedicated this silver unto the Lord from my hand to my son, to make a graven image and a molten image: now therefore I will restore it unto thee.*' Micah's mother was also a liar. She said that she was going to give the whole eleven hundred, then she only gave two hundred. This is typical of the worship of those who are outside God's truth and God's will. '*They made a graven image and a molten image, and they were in the house of Micah.'* (verse 4).

The ecumenical objective today is to put the faith of Christ among the other religions of the world. Christianity does not mix with any other religion. It stands totally in isolation. Christ is the intolerant Christ. *'No man cometh unto the Father but by Me.'* John 14:6. If you do not come by Jesus Christ you do not come at all. He is the only way to God. There is no such thing as a mixture of religions. There is one religion, true religion, and one true religion only.

A Corrupted Priesthood

In verse 9 we find a corrupted priesthood. Micah says, 'Well, it would be better if I had a priest.' The tribe of Levi was a priestly tribe, so he found this wanderer and made him his priest. Now, instead of the Levite saying, 'I will not be your priest. I am not going to be an idolator. I am not going to serve in a house of gods, in a tabernacle of idols', we find that this man of the priestly tribe of Levi, who should have been at Shiloh doing God's work in God's house, was prepared to become a priest in a pantheon of gods.

The priesthood corrupted! How corrupt today are the ministers of our land! How corrupt today are the clergy of our land! How corrupt today are the ecclesiastical leaders of our land! They seek to mix pure Christianity with paganism, popery, ecumenism and all the isms which have crawled through the grating of the pit to curse and debauch this evil age in which we live. No words of mine could be strong enough to denounce the corruption which we have today among the church leaders of our land!

Corrupted Faith

In verse 13 we find corrupted faith. Micah says, *'Now know I that the Lord will do me good.'* After breaking the crystal clear commandments of the Book he takes God's name upon his lips and says, *'Now know I that the Lord will do me good.'*

It is like the modern charismatic movement and their followers who profess that they are led by the Holy Spirit of God. ₍I was reading one of their books recently. In it one of the converts to the charismatic movement said that he went to a Protestant Pentecostal Church, he had hands laid on him, he spoke in tongues and as a result he loved Mary more than ever before, he enjoyed the mass as he never enjoyed it before, he lit more candles than he ever lit before. He was a more devoted Romanist than ever he was before. That is the deception of the Antichrist. If a man is genuinely worked upon by the Holy Spirit of God he flees from idolatry. He turns his back on the whole corrupt system of the Antichrist. He will have no part or lot with evil. He will stand for this Book in all its clarity and in all its truth. We are living in an age of corruption like the age in the Book of Judges.

We have looked at corrupted morals in verse 2, corrupted religion in verse 5, corrupted priesthood in verse 9, and corrupted faith in verse 13. Finally we must look at corruption in the family.

Corrupted Families

In chapter 18 you will discover corruption in a whole tribe, the tribe of Dan.

When I read chapter 18 I wondered why the tribe of Dan apostatised to idolatry so readily. Then I went back and found that the tribe of Dan refused to keep God's command to cast the enemy out from the territory in which they were placed.

Moses the man of God divided the whole land for the tribes, and every tribe had a special part of the heritage of the land flowing with milk and honey. Dan did not take up his position, he did not drive out the enemy, and as a result he became a wanderer in Israel.

When you do not take up the inheritance of the Lord and do not do the will of God you will be a prey to the enemy, the great enemy of our souls, Satan himself. Dan became a prey and here we find the children of Dan wandering

If you look at chapter 18:20 you will find moral corruption. The priest who was set over the house of Micah, the tribe of Dan, says 'Why be a priest to a family when you can be a priest to a whole tribe?' What did the priest do? *'And the priest's heart was glad, and he took the ephod, and the teraphim, and the graven image, and went in the midst of the people.'* The family started its road to corruption by thieving. Now we have a priest and he is thieving. He thieves the gods of Micah because he is morally corrupt and has no integrity.

There is one thing that makes me fear for Ulster, and that is that the Protestant people of this land are losing their integrity. There was a time when Ulster Protestants were known for their integrity. They were known for their integrity in business, their word was their bond. They were known for their integrity in personal relationships, but today there is a philosophy among Protestant people, 'Oh, if Roman Catholics can get away with it, why shouldn't I get away with it, and if Romanists break the law and get away with it, why shouldn't I break the law and get away with it?' That is the most dangerous element in our society today, and it could cause the overthrow of our Protestant heritage in these six counties. The corruption and corroding of living in a society that is Godless, Christless, and against the keeping of God's law, is rubbing off on the Protestant community to our shame. We must confess it! That is why we need a spiritual revival.

The Corruption of Religion

If you look at verse 17 you will find the corruption of religion. *'The five men that went to spy out the land went up and came in thither, and took the graven image, and the ephod, and the teraphim, and the molten image: and the priest stood at the entering of the gate with the six hundred men that were appointed with weapons of war.'* Here we have the corruption religiously, and the longing of this tribe to go over to idolatry.

In verse 31 you have the corruption of the whole priesthood, *'And they set them up Micah's graven image which he had made, all the time that the house of God was in Shiloh.'* Here was a new religion. God's religion was at Shiloh. Man's religion was here in the tribe of Dan. *'And Jonathan, the son of Gershom, the son of Manasseh, he and his sons were priests to the sons of Dan until the day of the captivity of the land.'* (v.30)

It is most interesting to note that this idolatry never ceased in Israel, not even when David reigned. Even when Solomon reigned there was idolatry in Dan, and until the day that they were led into captivity and taken to Babylon this idolatry persisted.

Is not that just like this country of ours? Did you ever know any nation on the face of God's earth whose history is parallel to the history of Israel as this nation of ours? There was a day when this nation was delivered from idolatry, a day when we had men who paid the price in sacrifice. The five martyred Bishops, Cranmer, Latimer, Ridley, Ferrar, and

Hooper, were burned at the stake to deliver this land from idolatry, but the idolatry still persists.

What happened to the tribe that persisted in its idolatry? Turn to Revelation 7 and you will find that this is the only tribe that is not mentioned when God calls the roll in Heaven. Idolatry put the tribe of Dan into Hell, and it is the only member of the family of Jacob which has no place in Heaven. Idolatry must be opposed, rejected and fought with all the vigour that we can muster.

When we turn to the last three chapters of Judges we go down into the very depths. You will see the darkness of homosexuality in this 19th chapter. It took a dramatic occurrence to stir the sleeping conscience of a corrupted society, and it was only when that man took the murdered body of his wife and cut her in twelve pieces and sent the pieces round the coasts of Israel that the people were alerted. What, I wonder, will awaken the consciences of the people of Ulster?

When you look at chapter 20 you will find the terrible judgment when the tribe of Benjamin was almost annihilated. The tribe of Dan, which was destroyed by idolatry, and the tribe of Benjamin which was devastated by sodomy, both go hand in hand.

Thank God the King is coming!

When we go over into the Book of Samuel we read of God's anointed man, King David. He came to deal with idolatry and sodomy.

Thank God we can conclude the exposition of this Book with these words, 'The King is coming,' and today my eye is on the coming of the Prince of Peace. Soon shall the trumpet sound. Soon shall angels crowd around His chariot. Soon shall Heaven's doors open, and there shall come forth from the Majesty of the Everlasting God His Wonderful Son, King of kings and Lord of lords. Then shall the knowledge of God cover the earth as the waters cover the sea, and the kingdoms of this world shall become the kingdoms of our Lord and of His Christ, and He shall reign!

Until the trumpet sounds may we be found with sword unsheathed, standing on the front line for God, refusing to surrender the principles of this Book, and earnestly contending for the faith once for all delivered to the saints.

May God help us, in Jesus' Name.

THE
⋙ IAN R. K. PAISLEY LIBRARY ⋘

OTHER BOOKS IN THIS SPECIAL SERIES

♦ Christian Foundations

♦ An Exposition of the Epistle to the Romans

♦ The Garments of Christ

♦ Sermons on Special Occasions

♦ Expository Sermons

♦ A Text a Day Keeps the Devil Away

♦ The Rent Veils at Calvary

♦ My Plea for the Old Sword

♦ Into the Next Millennium

♦ Sermons with Startling Titles

♦ Grow Old Along With Me

♦ For Such A Time As This